macO Sonoma User Guide

The Master Manual For Beginners And Seniors On How To Use MacBook Air And MacBook Pro With macOS 14 Tips And Tricks

Nolan Foman

Copyright © 2023 All rights reserved.

No part of this book shall be reproduced, stored in a retrieval system, or transmitted by any means, electronic, mechanical, photocopying, recording, or otherwise, without written permission from the publisher. Although every precaution has been taken in the preparation of this book, the publisher and author assume no responsibility for errors or omissions. Nor is any liability assumed for damages resulting from the use of the information contained herein.

LEGAL NOTICE:

This book is copyright protected and is only for personal use. This book should not be amended or distributed, sold, quote, or paraphrased without the consent of the author or publisher.

DISCLAIMER:

The information contained in this book is for educational purposes only. All efforts have been executed to present accurate, reliable, and up to date information. No warranties of any kind are implied. The contents from this book are derived from various sources. Please consult a licensed professional before attempting any techniques contained herein.

By reading this document, the reader agrees that under no circumstances is the author responsible for any losses, direct or indirect, which are incurred as a result of the information contained in this book including errors, omissions, and inaccuracy

Table of Contents

CHAPTER 1 1

   Update to macOS Sonoma 1

   Backup Disks for Time Machine 2

   Time Machine back up 7

   Choose a Time Machine storage gadget 7

   Restore Mac from a backup 9

   Fix Missing Menu Bar Icons 13

   Mac's menu bar 16

   Status Menus 17

   Rearrange Dock items 17

   Personalize the Dock 19

   Set Mac to a bright or dark appearance 19

   Set Up Spotlight 21

   Preview Spotlight result 22

CHAPTER 2 25

   Modify Default Keyboard Shortcuts 25

   Make Custom Keyboard Shortcuts 26

   Shortcut activation for dictation 28

Turn on or off automatic dictation punctuation 29

Combine dictation and keyboard 29

Open the App in Launchpad 29

Use Launchpad to search for Apps 30

Rearrange Apps in Launchpad......................................31

Use Launchpad to create app folders........................... 32

Remove apps in Launchpad... 32

Launchpad Reset... 33

Use Split View for Mac...35

Adjust split screen... 36

Exit split-screen 36

CHAPTER 3 37

Use Apple Game Mode...37

Tweak Display Contrast 38

Enable Corrected Words Highlight............................. 38

Interactive widgets.. 39

Editing and removing widgets 40

Desktop Icons and Widgets sizes.................................41

Customize Widget Style 41

Show or Hide Widgets 41

How to Enable Stage Manager 42

Use stage manager to organize apps and windows 43

Customize Stage Manager 43

Hide or display Stage Manager 44

Adjust Stage Manager settings 44

Personalize wallpaper 45

CHAPTER 4 48

Pin Notes 48

Float Notes 48

How to import files to Notes 49

How to export Notes as PDF 50

Note Checklist 51

Include Tables to Notes 51

Sort Notes 53

Collaborate with Notes 53

Apple Note Tags 54

Lock Notes 55

CHAPTER 5 56

Start Siri with "Siri" 56

Set up an iCloud Account 56

View iCloud Space 58

How Do I Set a limit on iCloud Storage 58

Free Up iCloud Storage space 59

Use Universal Control between Macs 62

Disconnect Mac from other gadgets 63

Disable Universal Control 64

Organize desktop Manually 64

Desktop Stacks 65

CHAPTER 6 67

Spring-loaded folders..67

Activate and deactivate spring-loaded folders 68

Make spring-loaded folders quicker or slower............ 68

Organize Important folders in the sidebar.................. 69

Use tags to organize files and folder 70

Use decluttering tools 72

Delete duplicate Files 74

Use Smart Folders to group files..................................75

Set a folder's view 78

How to customize folder View 78

CHAPTER 7 81

Share internet 81

Create Memoji 82

How to create a personal voice 84

Pause and restart personal voice recording 90

Create a focus 92

How to use focus 93

Customize Focus 93

Use Focus to Enable Contact Notifications 94

Set Apps Focus 98

Schedule .... Focus 100

Set Focus Filter 102

How to Synchronize Focus across gadgets 105

Configure Focus Status 105

CHAPTER 8 107

Activate Live Text 107

Use Live Text 107

Live Text Preview App 109

Video Live Text 110

Use Mac to Make and receive calls 111

Using Your Mac to Send and Receive Text 112

Set Up FaceTime On Mac 112

Make FaceTime call 114

Create a FaceTime Link 115

FaceTime Video Effects 116

FaceTime screen sharing 117

Change FaceTime Camera and Microphone 118

Set Screen Timeout 119

CHAPTER 9 121

Disable Screen Timeout 121

Explore screen-sharing app 122

End Screen Sharing 124

Use Video call reactions 124

Configure screen saver 127

How to Use Center Stage 128

Use Handoff 129

Switch on AirPlay 131

AirPlay from Mac to iOS Devices 131

AirPlay on TV with Mac 132

Listen to Podcasts 134

CHAPTER 10 137

Create Safari Tab Group 137

View All Safari tabs group 138

Rearrange Tab Groups 139

Remove a Tabs Group 139

Customize Safari toolbar 139

Pick another search engine 140

Create PDF Web pages 141

Safari Reading list 142

Safari reader 143

Customize Safari's Icon 143

Set Safari Background photo 144

Safari Homepage customization 145

Safari Bookmarks Folders 145

Set up Safari Profiles 146

Set another Safari Profile 146

How to use Safari Profiles 147

Deleting Your Safari Profile 148

Lock Safari Private tabs 148

Unlocking Safari private browsing 149

Remove website tracking identifiers 150

CHAPTER 11 151

Create Template Reminders 151

Use Reminders template 152

Share Reminders Template 152

How to use Shopping reminders 152

How to use Zoom Presenter Overlay 155

Adjust the Presenter Overlay's size and position 156

Keynote Slide Transitions 157

How to animate Keynote slides 158

Keynote Magic Move 159

Edit Keynote Slide layouts 161

Customize keynote toolbar 163

CHAPTER 12 165

Safari Web apps 165

Check Mac CPU Temperatures 166

Set up Hot Corners.. 167

Link AirPods to Mac... 169

Modify AirPods settings 171

Activate Find My Location Services 172

Activate Find My 173

Use Find My for friends and family 174

Use Find My for gadgets 176

Search items with Find My 176

CHAPTER 1

Update to macOS Sonoma

The newest release of macOS Sonoma can be obtained and set up using Software Update.

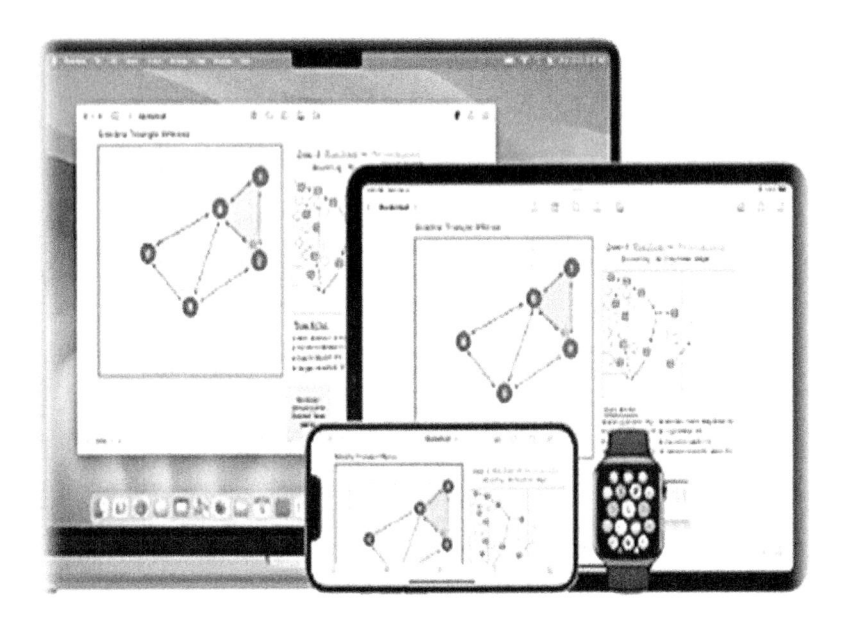

- Select System Settings from the Apple menu in the top left. After selecting General in the menu bar, select Software Update on the right.
- If you're using an older version of macOS, choose Software Update from the Apple menu > System Preferences.

- You can also access "Software Update" by searching for it in Spotlight and clicking on the result.

If your Mac is too old to have Software Update, you can still get macOS Sonoma from the App Store.

Backup Disks for Time Machine

You'll need one of these storage devices if you want to utilize Time Machine to back up your Mac.

1. External Disk attached to your Mac.
2. Support for Apple's Time Machine via Server Message Block (SMB) on a NAS.
3. Mac shared as Time Machine backups.
4. External drive linked to an AirPort Extreme AP (802.11ac) or AirPort Time Capsule.
5. Airport Time capsule.

External drive linked to Mac

- If you are using an external drive attached to your Mac through USB, Thunderbolt, or FireWire, Time Machine will automatically back it up. Time Machine will suggest formatting the disk if it detects an incompatible format.

Use a shared Mac as Time Machine backups

Follow these instructions on another Mac to set it up as a Time Machine backup target.

macOS Ventura or After

- Select the Apple menu > Pick System Preferences on the Mac you wish to use as a Time Machine backup.
- In the sidebar press General, then Choose Sharing on the right side.
- Switch on file sharing. Your administrator password may be required.
- To learn more about File Sharing, choose the info icon.
- Time Machine backups can be created by clicking the plus sign (+) next to the Shared Folders list and selecting a destination folder.
- Select Advanced Options from the menu that displays when you control-click the newly created folder.
- Choose "Share as a Time Machine backup destination," and then confirm with OK.

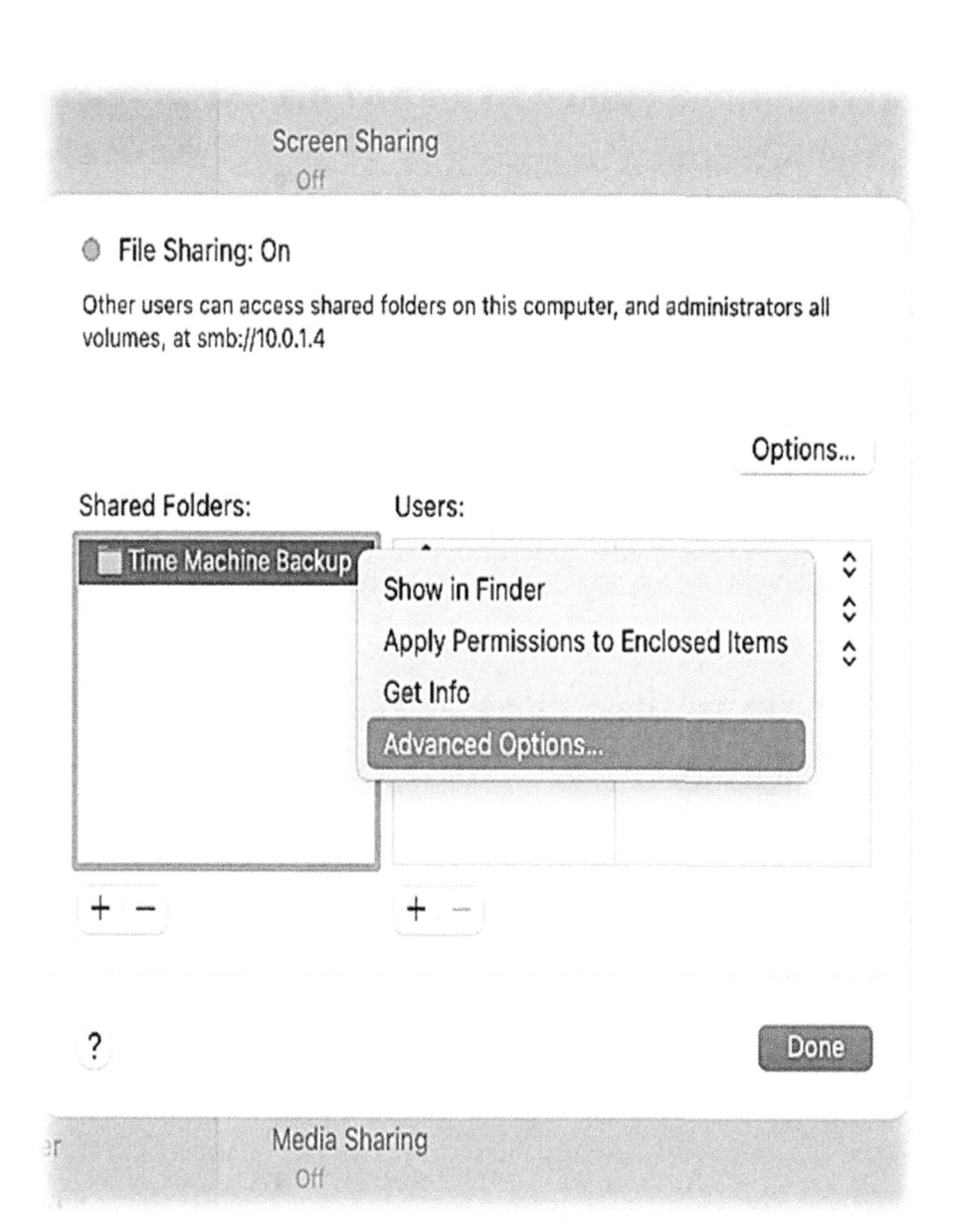

Time Machine on your other Macs should now recognize the shared folder and allow you to use it as a backup drive.

External drive Linked to an AirPort Extreme Base or AirPort Time Capsule

If you have an AirPort Extreme Base Station (802.11ac type) or an AirPort Time Capsule, Time Machine can be applied for back up to an external USB drive.

- Plug it straight into your Mac, and then with Disk Utility you can erase it.
- Activate your AirPort base station and plug the drive into one of its USB ports.
- To change the settings on your base station, launch AirPort Utility, then click the Edit button next to the station's name.
- In the configuration window, choose the Disks tab.
- Click "Enable file sharing" after choosing your backup drive from the partition list.
- Enter the settings window and press the Disks tab
- To prevent other users on the network from accessing your backups while using Time Machine, choose "Secure Shared Disks" from the Time Machine preferences menu. To add users, choose "With accounts" from the drop-down box and then tap the plus sign (+).

- When you're ready to implement the settings, click Update to restart the base station.

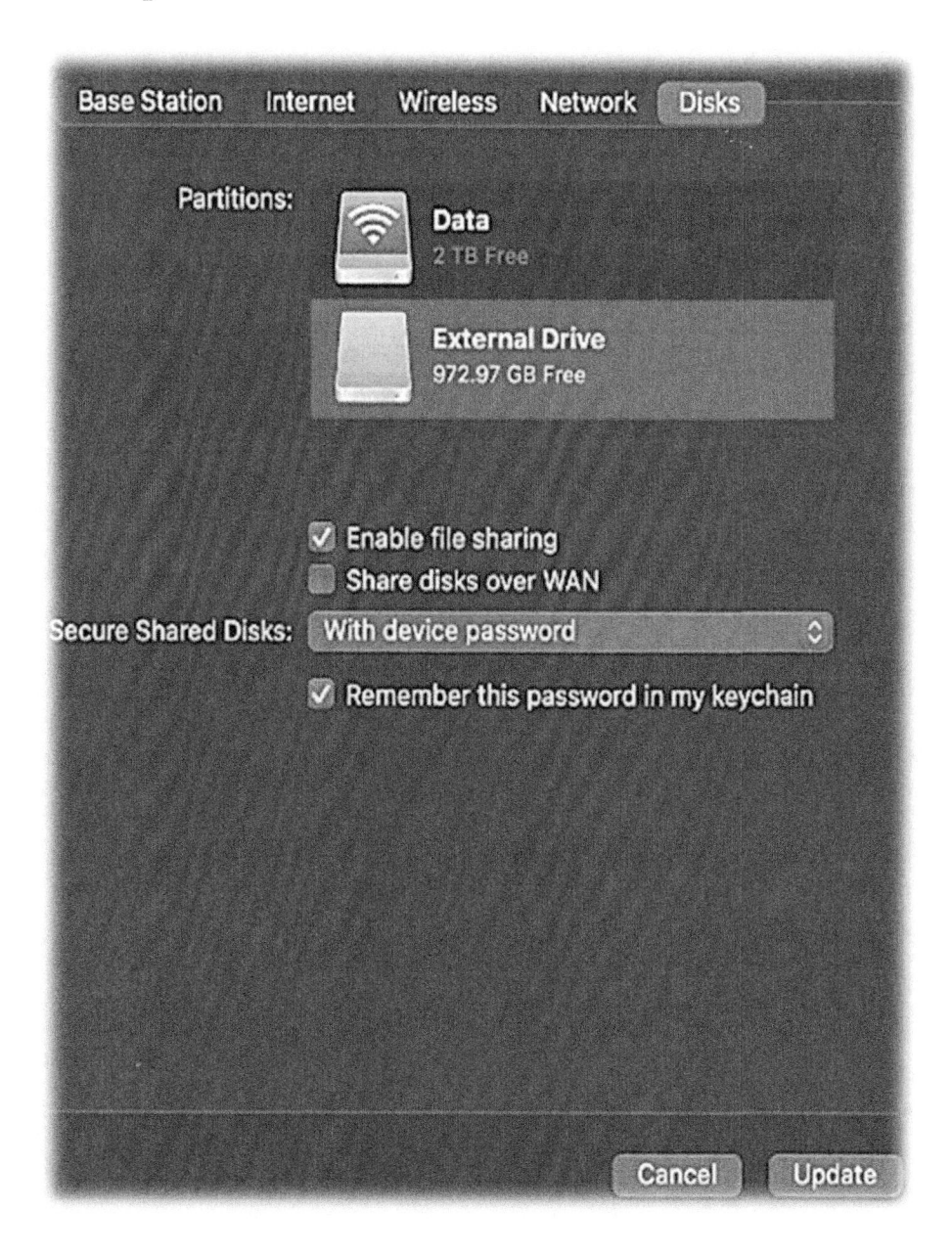

Time Machine back up

Link storage device for backup

Plug in a USB or Thunderbolt drive to your Mac to access external storage. Or you might find out about other backup drive options for Time Machine.

- This disk is for Time Machine backups exclusively and should not be used for any other purpose.
- A good rule of thumb is to have a backup drive with double the capacity of each disk or volume you back up. Time Machine will warn you if your backup drive is too small to hold a full backup.

Choose a Time Machine storage gadget

Your Mac may prompt you to utilize the storage for Time Machine backups when you link the device. If it doesn't prompt you to, do as follows.

- Launch the Time Machine settings:
- To access Time Machine, choose it from the Apple menu > System Settings > General > Time Machine.
- Choose the external drive for back up in Time Machine's settings.

- To add anything, just hit the plus sign (+) and do what it says.
- You can be prompted to "claim" existing backups from another Mac's Time Machine if the storage device already includes backups from that computer. Alternately, you can initiate a brand-new backup.

Make a backup

Back up Automatically. When you configure Time Machine to back up to a specific device, it will immediately begin doing so at regular intervals.

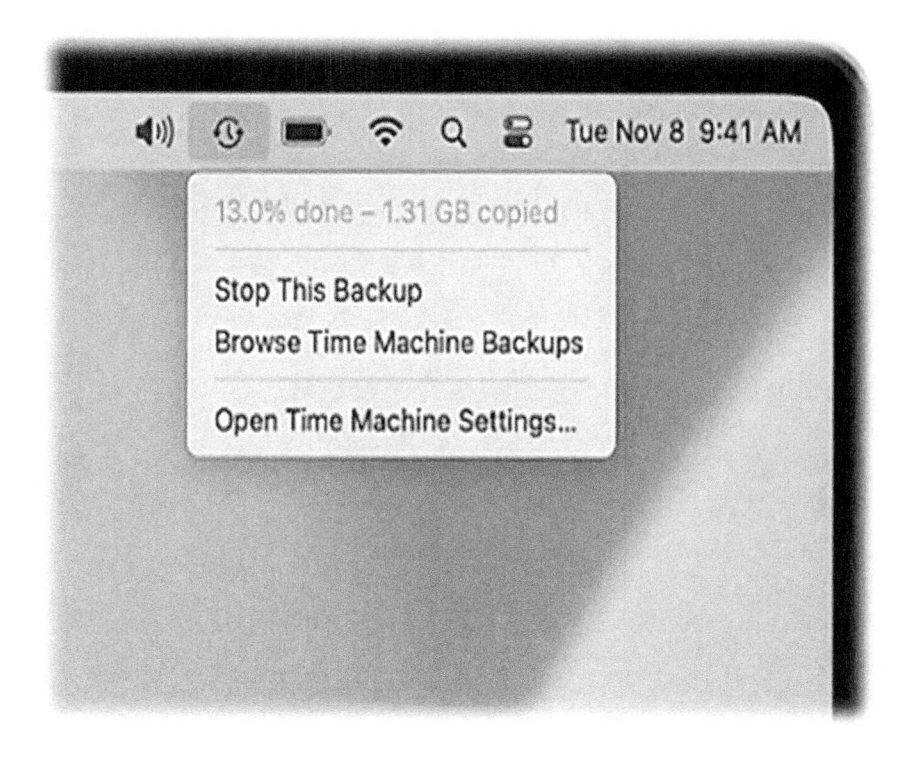

Manual Back up. Select Back Up Now from Time Machine's main menu to initiate a backup immediately rather than waiting for another scheduled backup.

Check the backups status. To see how far along a backup is or to stop it altogether, choose Time Machine from the menu bar. If a backup is currently running, for instance, the menu will reflect its progress. The time and date of the most recent backup are shown in the menu if a backup is not currently in progress.

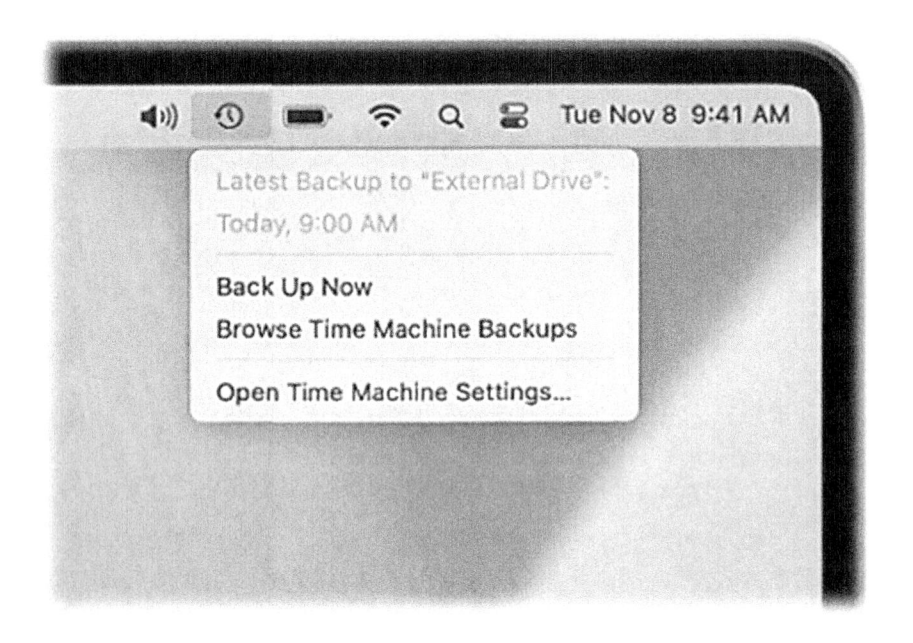

Restore Mac from a backup

To restore data on your Mac from a Time Machine backup, use the Migration Assistant.

Use Migration Assistant

- Before you continue, you should reinstall macOS if you need to. For instance, if you see a blinking question mark when you boot up your Mac, you should reinstall macOS.
- Be sure that Mac is linked with Time Machine back up disk.
- Launch the Mac's Migration Assistant. It's in the Applications folder, under Utilities.

The setup assistance on your Mac may contain a migration helper if it prompts you for information upon startup, such as your nation and network.

- When prompted to choose a method for transferring data, you can choose to use a Mac, a Time Machine, or a startup disk. Just hit the "Continue" icon.
- You can continue after choosing your Time Machine backup.
- Pick a backup, then hit continue.

Migration Assistant

If you have information on another Mac or a Windows PC, you can transfer it to this Mac. You can also transfer information from a Time Machine backup or another startup disk.

How do you want to transfer your information?

○ From a Mac, Time Machine backup or Startup disk
　From a Windows PC
　To another Mac

- Choose the info to move.
- Please read the following explanation of account transfers before clicking the Continue button.

Transfer information to this Mac

Choose which backup to transfer information from.

John's MacBook Pro

> Media (Macintosh HD – Data)
　Last Backup: July 28, 2020

> Media (Macintosh HD – Data)
　Last Backup: Today at 9:41:00 AM

11

John Appleseed is a user account in this illustration. Migration Assistant prompts you to rename or replace a Mac account with the same name.

Select the information to transfer

Choose which information you'd like to transfer to this Mac

☑ Applications		2.5 MB
☑ John Appleseed		13.49 GB
☑ Other Files & Folders		766.7 MB
☑ System & Network		44 KB

14.26 GB selected, about 677.52 GB available after transferring.

1. **Rename:** After you change the name, the Time Machine account will show up as a new user on your Mac, complete with their own login and home directory.

2. **Replace:** When you restore from a Time Machine backup, the account it contains will replace the one with the same name on your Mac.

- It might take many hours for a large transfer to finish, and there could be brief pauses along the way. You might begin in the evening and give the migration process the whole night to finish. To begin the transfer, choose Continue.
- After Migration Assistant has finished, you can access the transferred account's files by logging into that account on your Mac.

Fix Missing Menu Bar Icons

If the icons in the navigation bar are obscured or missing from your home screen, try the solutions provided below. In order to find a solution, you must focus on every possibility.

1 First, see control center settings

The very first thing you should do is look at the menus in the control hub. In most cases, the absence of the control center menu indicates that the user has chosen to hide it from view in the Mac's preferences. If the OS menu bar settings have been deactivated in macOS Sonoma, you will need to refresh the OS menu bar settings and then enable them again. I'll tell you what to do.

- To access the Control Panel, go to the System settings.
- The Wi-Fi and Bluetooth network connections menus can be found here.
- Select "Don't Show in Menu Bar" from the context menu that appears when you mouse over "Wi-Fi" or "Bluetooth."
- After waiting a moment, pick "Show in Menu Bar" from the drop-down option.

After making your choice, return to the home display to see whether the menu bar icon has shown. In case the problem still exists, try the following steps.

2 Restart Your Mac in Safe Mode

For others who have also had this problem with macOS Sonoma, restarting into safe mode has been recommended. Safe mode can be used to troubleshoot macOS Sonoma without worrying about installing malicious software or third-party programs. If you find that the icons for the menu bar are gone from your macOS desktop, you can force a restart into safe mode. Since this process deletes all transient data and caches, utilizing it is completely safe.

If you want to restart your Mac in safe mode, you can do so as follows:

- Click the Apple icon in the upper left corner then choose power down.
- In the new window that has opened, choose the Shut Down option once again.
- The Mac will power down automatically.
- Hold on for 10 secs.
- To activate your Mac, hold the power button for just a few seconds.
- Your device's logo should load, and you'll be prompted to choose a startup disk.
- At some point, a login window will appear when you hit and hold the Shift key on your keyboard.
- You will need to manually input the password you use to unlock your Mac every time you want to log in.
- Now that you're in safe mode, you can view whether the menu bar appears.

3: Reset Your system Settings

The issue you're seeing with the menu bar icons on macOS Sonoma can be resolved by resetting the Mac's system settings. Your Mac will be completely wiped clean in no time. Here is how to force the Mac to go back to factory settings.

- Use the Apple menu in the top left corner of the display to access System Preferences.
- The "Erase All Content & Settings" option can be found in the computer's settings menu.
- After that, click the OK button on the Mac Erase Assistant password window after entering your admin passcode.
- Press the Continue icon one again.
- Once you've signed out of your Apple ID, choose "Erase All Content & Settings" and confirm.

Mac's menu bar

- On a Mac, you'll find the menu bar at the top of the display. To choose actions, complete tasks, and see progress, use the menus and icons on the top bar.
- The Apple menu and app menus can be seen on the left side of the display. Spotlight, Control Center, Siri,

and the Notification Center can all be found on the right side of the display.

Status Menus

Towards the menu bar's right end, you'll find items also identified as status menus, with symbols that provide information about your Mac, such as its battery life and the ability to adjust settings like the keyboard's brightness.

- A status menu icon can be clicked to provide further information or settings.
- To see a list of accessible wireless networks, choose Wi-Fi; to toggle Dark Mode or Night Shift, select Display. The menu bar's visibility is entirely within your control.

You can rearrange the icons in the status menu by holding down the Command key and dragging them around. Quickly get rid of a status menu by dragging its icon out of the menu bar while you press down the Command key.

Rearrange Dock items

Insert item to Dock: To make room for less-recently used applications, move them to the left side of the line separating them. You can organize your recently used applications by dragging and dropping files and folders to the right side. The object gets given a new name in the Dock.

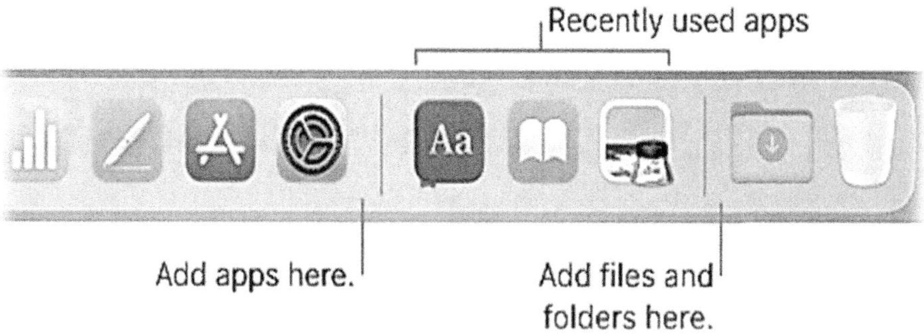
Recently used apps
Aa
Add apps here.
Add files and folders here.

You can see your folders stacked when you shift them to the Dock. The Dock normally has a Downloads folder. For more details on how to make use of the Dock's folders, go here.

To get rid of an item in the Dock, just drag it out of the Dock until the Remove button appears. The original file or folder remains on your Mac's hard drive; only the alias is deleted.

An app icon can be quickly and easily restored to the Dock if it is unintentionally deleted. Launch the program to restore its Dock icon. Select Options > Keep in Dock by Control-clicking the app's icon.

- Move an item to a new Dock slot by dragging it there.

Personalize the Dock

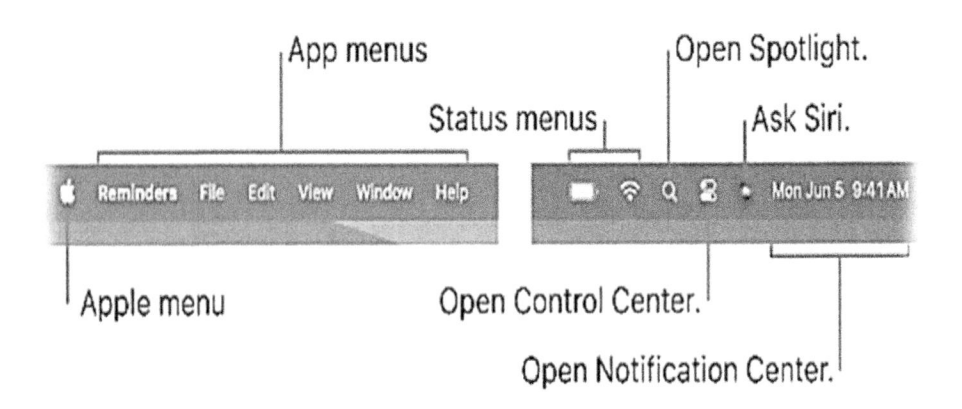

```
App menus                    Open Spotlight.
         Status menus        Ask Siri.
[menu bar image]
Apple menu      Open Control Center.
                Open Notification Center.
```

- To modify your Mac's desktop and dock, pick Apple menu > System Settings. Please scroll down if necessary.
- Alter the settings to your liking below Dock on the right.

The Dock's appearance, size, position relative to the screen's edges, and even its visibility are all modifiable.

Set Mac to a bright or dark appearance

You can manually switch between a bright and dark theme for your Mac's menu bar, Dock, windows, and built-in programs, or set your Mac to do it automatically.

- Access the Mac's Appearance preferences through the Apple menu > System Settings > Appearance. Please scroll down if necessary.
- On the right, click Light, Dark, or Auto.
1. Light is an unchanging appearance of light.
2. A dark appearance does not alter with time. In Dark Mode, the interface's colors are dimmed, drawing attention to the content you're editing while making the windows and controls disappear. Documents, presentations, pictures, videos, web sites, and more can all be viewed with ease.

A helpful hint is that you can toggle Dark Mode on and off using the Control Center. Select Dark Mode from the menu bar's Control Center, followed by Display.

- When Night Shift time comes around, the look will automatically transition from bright to dark. The instructions for doing so can be found under Night Shift Settings.
- If your Mac has been inactive for more than a minute, or if an app is keeping the display from resting (for example, during media playing), Auto won't change the look until the program is no longer active.

Set Up Spotlight

- Spotlight's initial settings can be accessed through the Apple menu via System Preferences. Choose Siri and Spotlight.
- Pressing CMND+SPACE in older versions of macOS brings up a Spotlight window. In macOS Ventura, the same shortcut now summons Siri to do a search through voice control.
- To restore the default behavior of the CMND+SPACE keyboard shortcut, choose the Keyboard Shortcut option and toggle it off or to another shortcut.

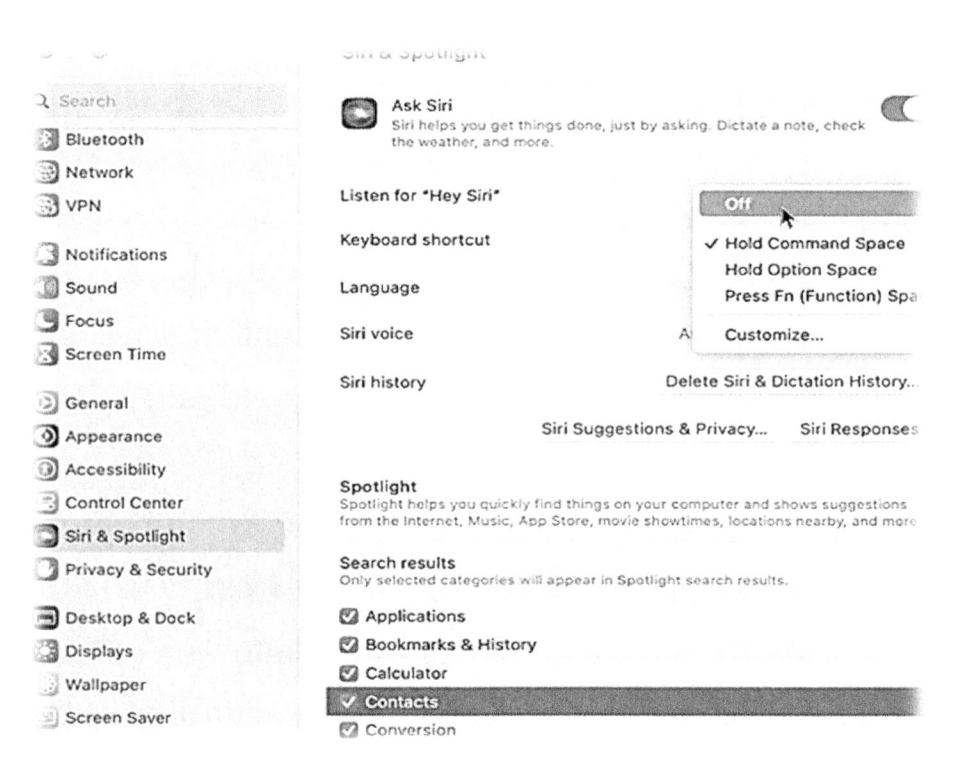

- The results of your Spotlight search should appear below; evaluate them all. You can disable the ones you don't want to show up, but it's recommended to keep them all checked for the time being.
- You can launch Spotlight by clicking the search symbol in the menu bar or, if you modified the shortcut's actions in System settings, click CMND+SPACE. Start your search by entering a keyword or phrase into the Spotlight Search box.
- Web pages, photos, applications, and files, as well as emails, messages, calendar appointments, and contacts, can all be given in a search, depending on the term.

You can use the Mac's Quick Look feature to get a sneak peek at the search results for many of these file formats in a new window.

Preview Spotlight result

- Choose a result and hit the spacebar. If the outcome is not previewable, your Mac will indicate by making a "boop" noise. If a preview is available, further information about the outcome will appear in a Quick Look window. The preview window can be

closed or the result opened in the appropriate program.
- The next new feature is the ability to go straight to the desired activity or task after doing a search for it.

Simply enter the desired OS-related word, such as "add user" or "update software," into the Spotlight Search area. Start a search for "add user account" or "software update."

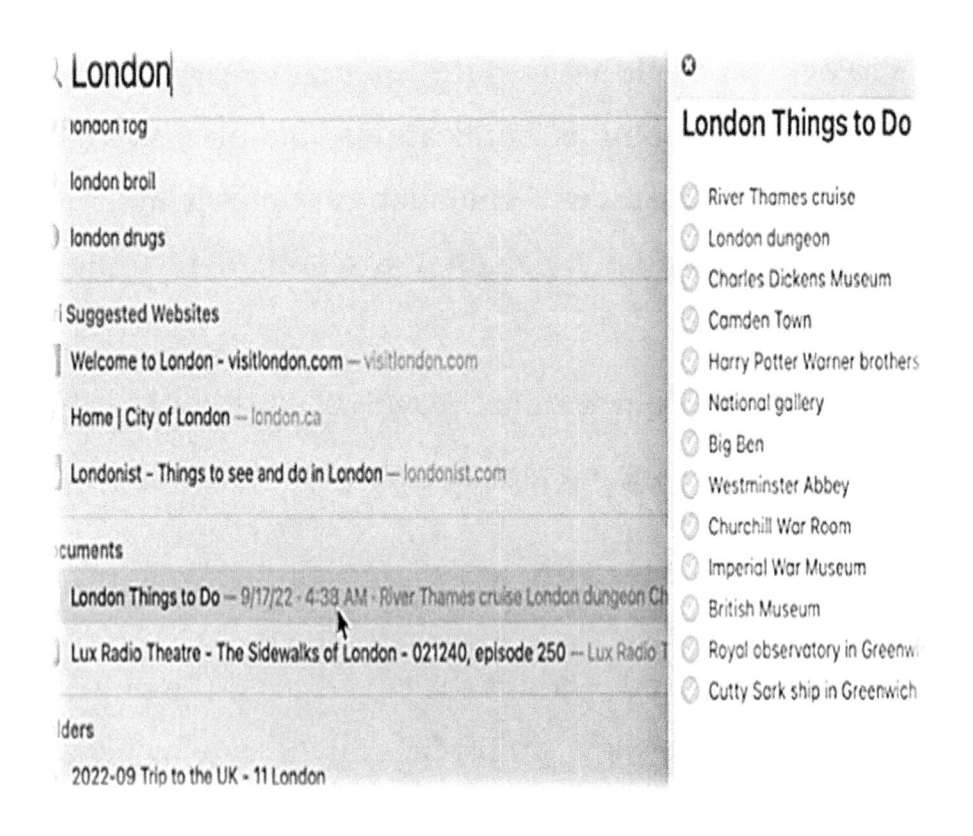

At last, you can get detailed information on things like performers, bands, films, TV series, companies, and sports teams. Without having to scour your Mac or the web, such results unearth a plethora of information about your search query. Enter the name of a subject from the list to see whether it works. Your desired result should be the first on the list. To examine the wide range of data available, click the first result

CHAPTER 2
Modify Default Keyboard Shortcuts

- In the menu bar, choose Apple > System Preferences.
- Select Keyboard from the menu that drops down.
- Select Keyboard Shortcuts on the right-hand side of the window.
- A new window will appear. The choices for customizing the shortcut keys appear on the left. Make your choice below.
- Keyboard shortcuts can be modified by double-clicking the existing shortcut next to the desired action and entering the desired new shortcut.

The checkboxes next to each action have checkmarks by default, but you can remove them if you choose. To modify the default keyboard shortcut for VoiceOver (Command + F5), open the left-hand menu and choose Accessibility; then, double-press the shortcut you want to alter. Then press whatever combination of keys you choose.

- When you're through making changes to your keyboard shortcuts, choose Done from the window's action menu. However, if you want to revert to the factory settings, you can do so by selecting Restore Defaults at the window's bottom.

Make Custom Keyboard Shortcuts

- Select Apple menu, System settings, then press Keyboard.
- On the right select Keyboard Shortcuts.
- In the new window, hit App Shortcuts from the sidebar on the left.
- Press the (+) sign under All apps.
- Select the program you want to provide a shortcut to by clicking All Applications.

We'll go with Mail, as we discussed before.

- In the space provided next to Menu Title, type the name of the menu item for which you want to set a shortcut.

It is crucial that you type it precisely as it appears in the app's menu. Since this is a shorthand for the Import Mailboxes menu item, the full title should read "Import Mailboxes."

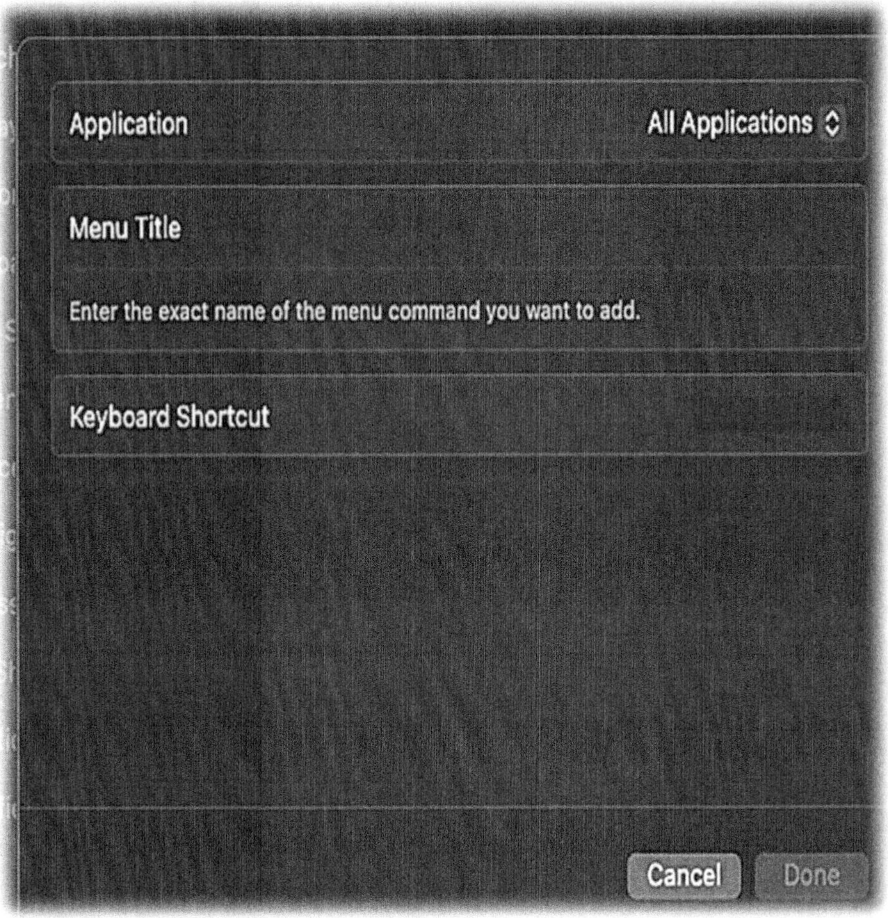
Application
All Applications
Menu Title
Enter the exact name of the menu command you want to add.
Keyboard Shortcut
Cancel
Done

- Close to Keyboard Shortcut, input your desired key combination.

Keep in mind that you must come up with a different combination each time. Your shortcut won't function on your Mac if the key combination is currently in use.

- Double-click the "Done" icon at the screen's bottom right to complete the process.

There are two methods to check whether you were successful. To perform the action for which you programmed the keyboard shortcut, you must first launch the application in question and go to the appropriate menu item. If the key combination you entered appears in the box, then the search was successful.

The alternative is to launch the program and test the new keyboard shortcut. If it's functional, you can begin using it. If it doesn't, check that you've typed the action name accurately and try again.

Shortcut activation for dictation

Dictation in macOS can be activated using many different keyboard keys.

- Select the desired shortcut by going to the System Settings app, then to the Keyboard, and then to the Dictation section.
- You can activate it in several ways, such as by pressing the microphone symbol, the globe icon twice, or the control key twice.

- To create your own shortcut for dictation if you don't like the ones provided, go to Options.

Turn on or off automatic dictation punctuation

You can choose to enable or deactivate automatic punctuation while using dictation.

- To enable or disable automatic punctuation, open System Settings, choose Keyboard, scroll down to the Dictation section, and tap the toggle there.

Combine dictation and keyboard

- Select System settings by clicking the Apple menu icon.
- Click Keyboard in the left pane's drop-down menu.
- To activate dictation, click the microphone icon under Dictation.

You can now speak words and they will display on the display.

Open the App in Launchpad

- Launchpad can be accessed in three different ways:
1. In your Dock, press the Launchpad icon.
2. Do a pinch gesture with all four fingers on your trackpad.

3. If using an Apple keyboard, press the Launchpad icon.
- To open an app, just click its icon.

Use Launchpad to search for Apps
- Open Launchpad.
- To begin a search, go to Launchpad's top-center search box.
- Simply type in the program's name and it will be shown.

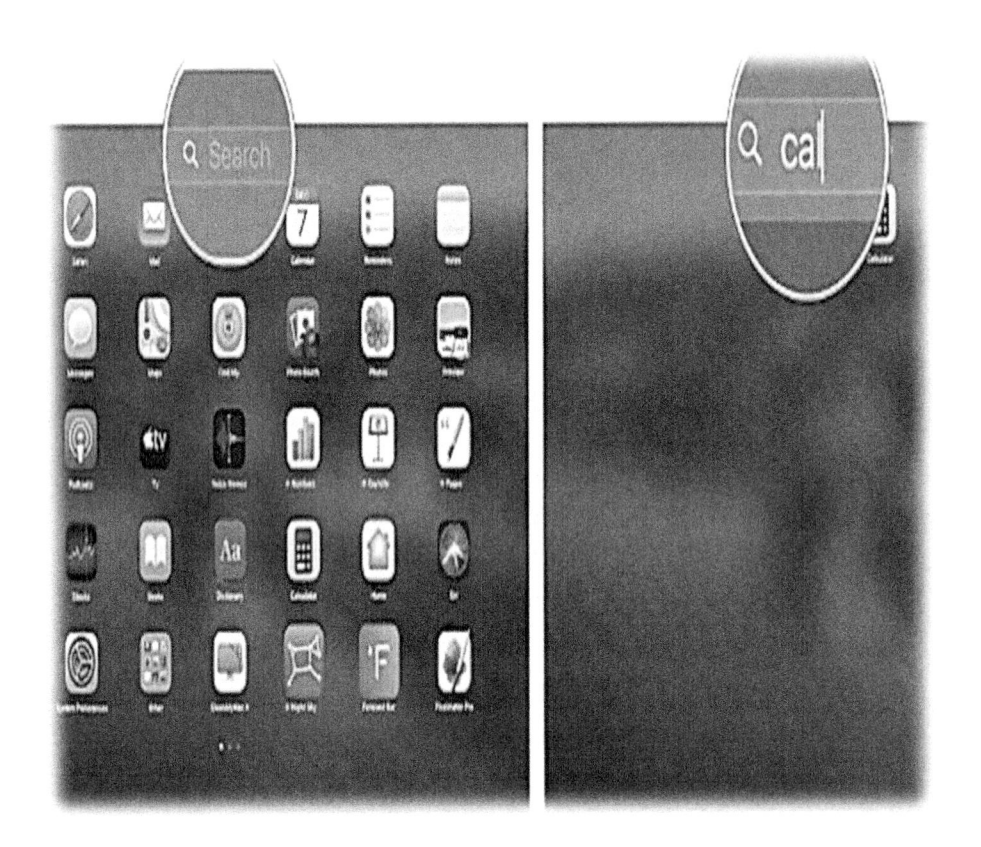

- Pick the app.

In most situations, you probably won't even need to input the whole name of the software to discover it since Launchpad will start results filtering as soon as you start typing.

Rearrange Apps in Launchpad
- Enter Launchpad.
- To wiggle an app, click and hold it until it begins to wiggle.

- Use the mouse to move the program.

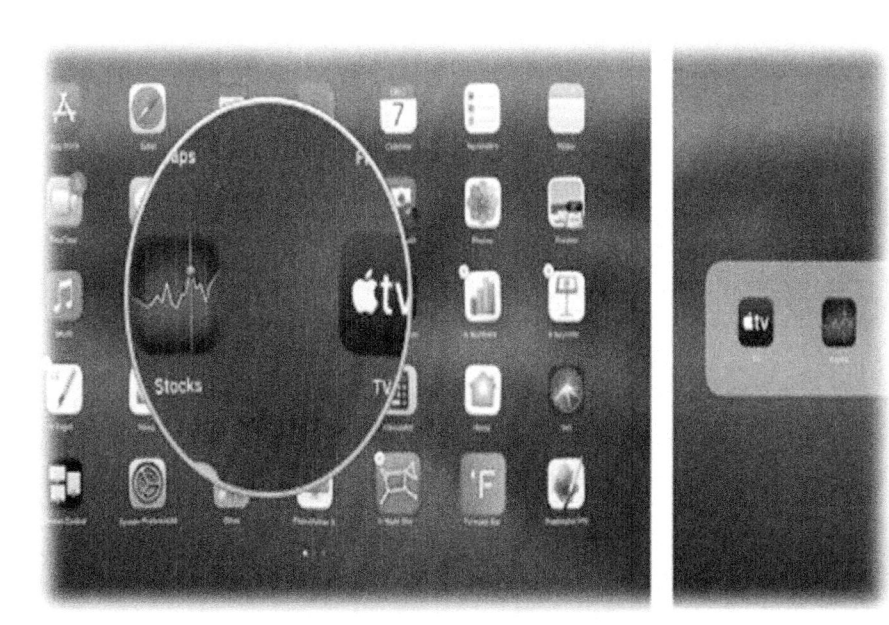

Use Launchpad to create app folders
- Enter Launchpad.
- To move an app to a folder, click and hold on it until it jiggles.
- To move an app into a certain folder, just drag it on top of the app you want to move into the same folder, then a white box will display. Drop the program into a preexisting folder.
- Let go.

Remove apps in Launchpad
- Enter Launchpad.

- To uninstall an app, just click and hold it until it begins to wiggle.
- To uninstall an app, tap the X in its upper right corner.
- In the resulting pop up, click Delete.

Launchpad Reset

- Press on a desktop.
- Choose Go. It's at the very top of your display, in the menu bar.
- Hold the Option key press for now.
- Press Library.
- Click the Application Support folder twice.
- Double-press the Dock folder.

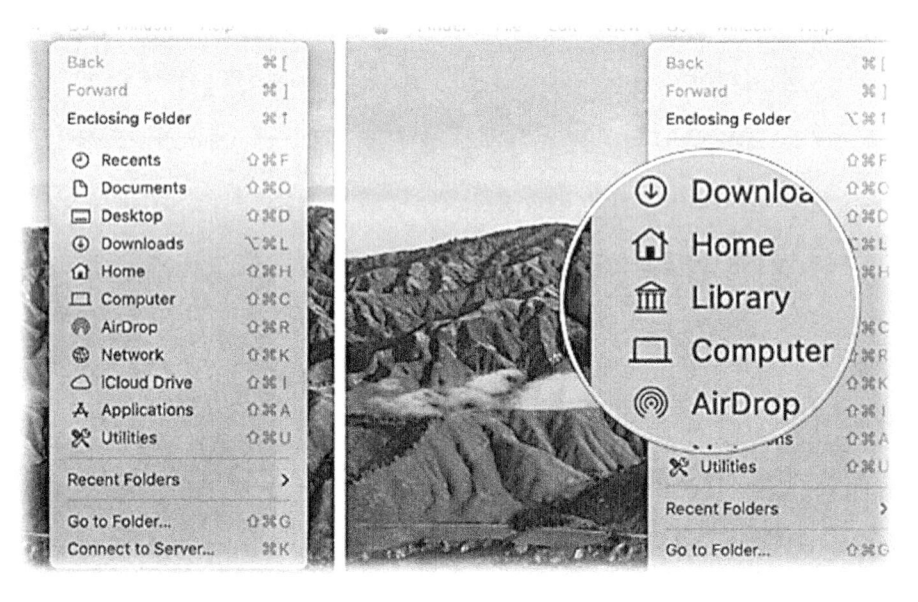

- Put any all.db files in the trash.
- Just click the Apple logo on the upper left edge. It ought to resemble this format.
- Press restart.

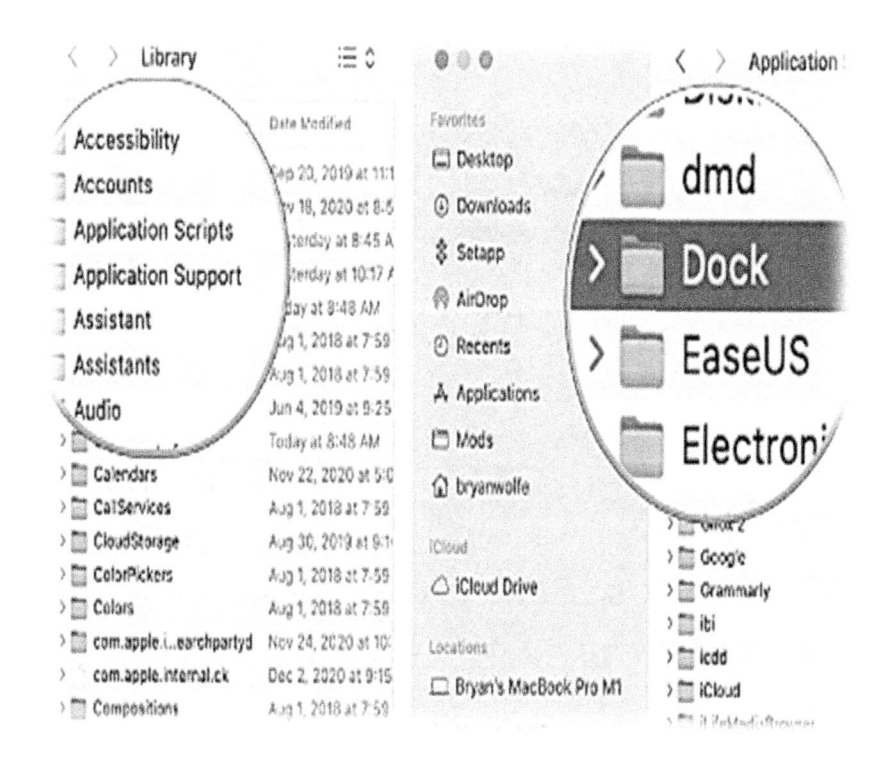

- Click the Restart icon again to confirm.
- Once the restart is complete, you should locate all of your programs in Launchpad.

Use Split View for Mac

- To activate the Split View mode, click the green button between the minimize and close icons on the toolbar.
- Pick either option of "Tile Window to Left of Screen" or "Tile Window to Right of Screen"
- To make two apps appear side by side, click on one on the left side of the display.

Adjust split screen

When using a Mac, the two windows you have side by side do not always need to be the same size. You are preparing a presentation and referring to a map; the presentation itself should occupy more vertical real estate than the map or your notes.

- Split View allows convenient adjustment on much display each program uses.
- To achieve this, just grab the vertical bar in the middle of the screen and move it. That's all; you can now scale the setup to whatever size you choose.
- You can also swap their positions by dragging one window to the other, which is a handy feature.

Exit split-screen

- When you're done using Split View, you can exit the dual-window mode by using the Esc key or by pressing the same green icon at the upper part of the display.

CHAPTER 3

Use Apple Game Mode

macOS Sonoma decides when to switch on and off Game Mode. You certainly have to be running a game. Full-screen games are required to activate Game Mode on macOS Sonoma. No controls or options are possible till then.

After expanding the game to fill the display, a controller icon appears in the Mac's menu bar. If you have a physical controller plugged in, you will still see that symbol.

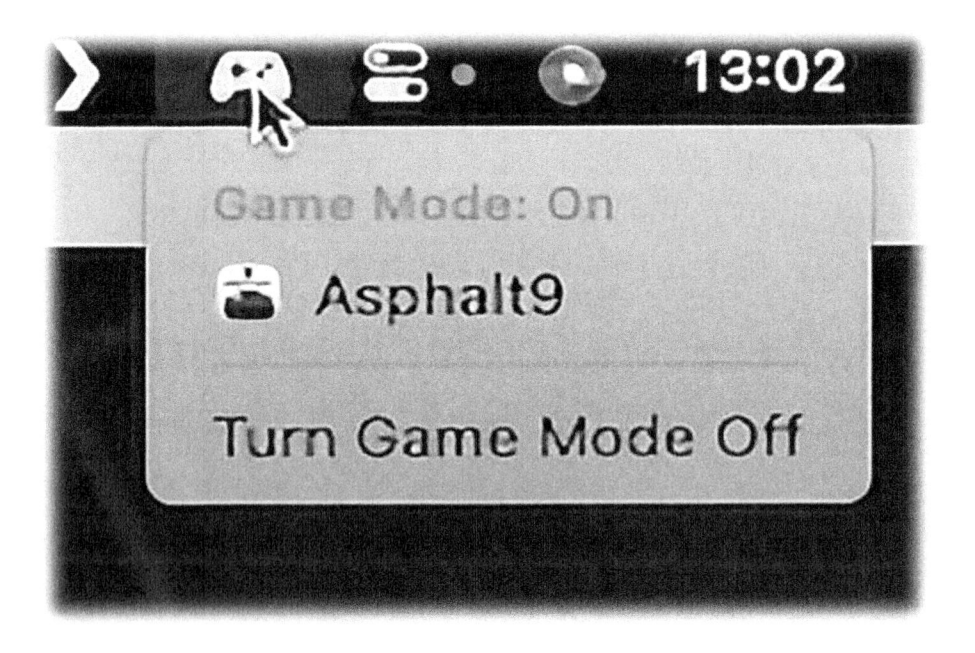

The app's menu in the menu bar will display the title of the currently playing game, followed by the option to "Turn Game Mode Off."

Tweak Display Contrast

Mac OS has always had the option to tweak the display's contrast, but it has never seemed so robust and user-friendly until now.

- If you want to change the contrast on your macOS device, open the System Preferences program, then to Accessibility, then Display, and finally click on the Display contrast slider.

Enable Corrected Words Highlight

- In the Apple menu, access System Preferences, enter Keyboard, press Edit, click All Input Sources, and then Input Method.
- Switch on predictive text inline.

Interactive widgets

The introduction of macOS Sonoma will give programmers time to make widgets more interactive, if necessary.

Until recently, a widget might provide data like the current temperature, the latest headlines, or the health of your HomeKit gadgets. If you click on a widget, it will take you to the app's main screen. That is still the case if you don't click properly. For instance, you can now toggle a light on or off with the press of a button on Apple's Home widget. The Home widget's buttons will indicate that you've turned on the light without launching the entire Home app.

Editing and removing widgets

- You can right-click on a widget to see what kind of customization options it provides. The widget will show the available choices if any exist.
- You can move a widget from its current location if you decide you don't like it there.
- Then, you can choose between two solutions if you just want to discard a widget. The widget can be deleted by right-clicking it and selecting "Remove Widget" from the context menu.

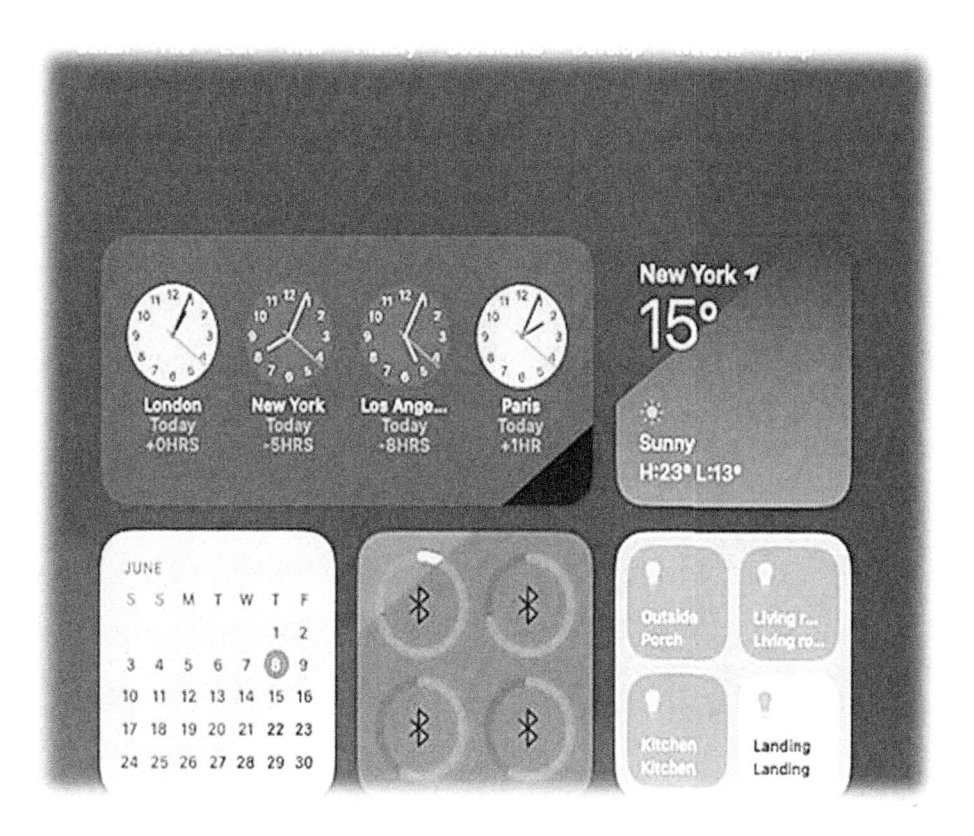

Alternately, you can right-click a blank area on your desktop and choose Edit Widgets. Just as when you originally added a widget, a delete icon will appear in the upper left corner of each widget you now have.

Desktop Icons and Widgets sizes

Changing the size of a desktop widget is usually the only modification that has to be made to it.

- Right/control- Click on a certain widget -> pick Edit Widget in the menu and then choose Small, Medium, or Large as per your desire.

Customize Widget Style

- Enter System Settings -> Desktop & Dock -> enter the Widgets section and click on the drop-down menu next to Widget Style.
- After that, pick Full-color, Automatic, or Monochrome.

Show or Hide Widgets

Your iPhone's widgets are synchronized with your Mac so you can utilize them to decorate your desktop in a coordinated fashion. However, you can disable syncing if you don't like the automatic updates or just want to keep your Mac's widgets library tidy.

- To disable the widgets, use the System Settings app and go to Desktop & Widgets > Desktop > Turn off Show Widgets.

Widgets will now be automatically hidden once a window for an app is opened. In addition, you can click on the background to make them invisible or visible.

- To always display the desktop widgets on your Mac, open the System Preferences program, go to Desktop & Widgets, click Desktop, and then activate the Show Widgets switch.

How to Enable Stage Manager

- To access the control center, move the mouse cursor to the top of the display.
- Then, open the Stage Manager by clicking on it.
- You'll see a window that describes Stage Manager and gives you the choice to activate it. A Stage Manager toggle switch.
- The Stage Manager can now be used. The currently active app will be front and center, with the other

applications shown on each side in their minimized states.

- Stage Manager can be added to the Menu Bar by toggling the Show in Menu Bar option in Settings > Control Center > Stage Manager.

Use stage manager to organize apps and windows

- The center window can be resized and relocated by dragging its title bar or its edge.
- Simply by dragging a thumbnail into the main window, you may create a new group of windows.
- Another option is to hold down the Shift key and click the thumbnail. A window can be detached from the group by shifting it to the side.
- Pressing Command-H will hide the app's thumbnail and any open windows.
- Pressing Command-Tab will bring up a previously hidden window.

Customize Stage Manager

- To move windows between stages, just click and drag the window. You can reposition windows anywhere you want on the stage.

- There are a few customization choices for each stage in the upper right edge. You can choose the wallpaper, background color, and the number of rows/columns in each individual level.
- Third, typing 'Cmd+Spacebar' on your keyboard will bring up Spotlight, your computer's search tool. Using the resulting search bar, which appears in the screen's upper-center, you can do a system-wide search of your Mac without leaving the current window.

Hide or display Stage Manager

The Stage Manager is on hand at all times in the Control Room. You can also choose to display it in the main menu.

- To access the Mac's Control Center, pick Apple menu > System Settings. (It may help to scroll below.)
- Press the displayed menu close to Stage Manager's on the right, visibility in the then pick display in the menu bar or don't display in the menu bar.

Adjust Stage Manager settings

- Select System Preferences from the Apple menu, and then select Desktop & Dock in the left pane. (It can help to scroll below.)

- On the right, choose Desktop and stage manager.
- Next to show items, mark or unmark checkboxes.

On desktop: Display desktop items.

In stage manager: When the stage manager is switched on, it will display desktop items.

If you disable this setting, your most frequently used applications will be hidden until you move the mouse cursor to the left side of the display.

- Press the click wallpaper to view the desktop box and pick the available options.
- Switch on and off stage manager.
- Switch on and off to show recent apps.
- You can likewise press show windows from an app.

Personalize wallpaper

- To change your desktop background on a Mac, pick the Apple menu > press System Settings > Wallpaper.
- You may change your desktop image by choosing one of the following:
- Any of the following can be done to alter a background image or color:

45

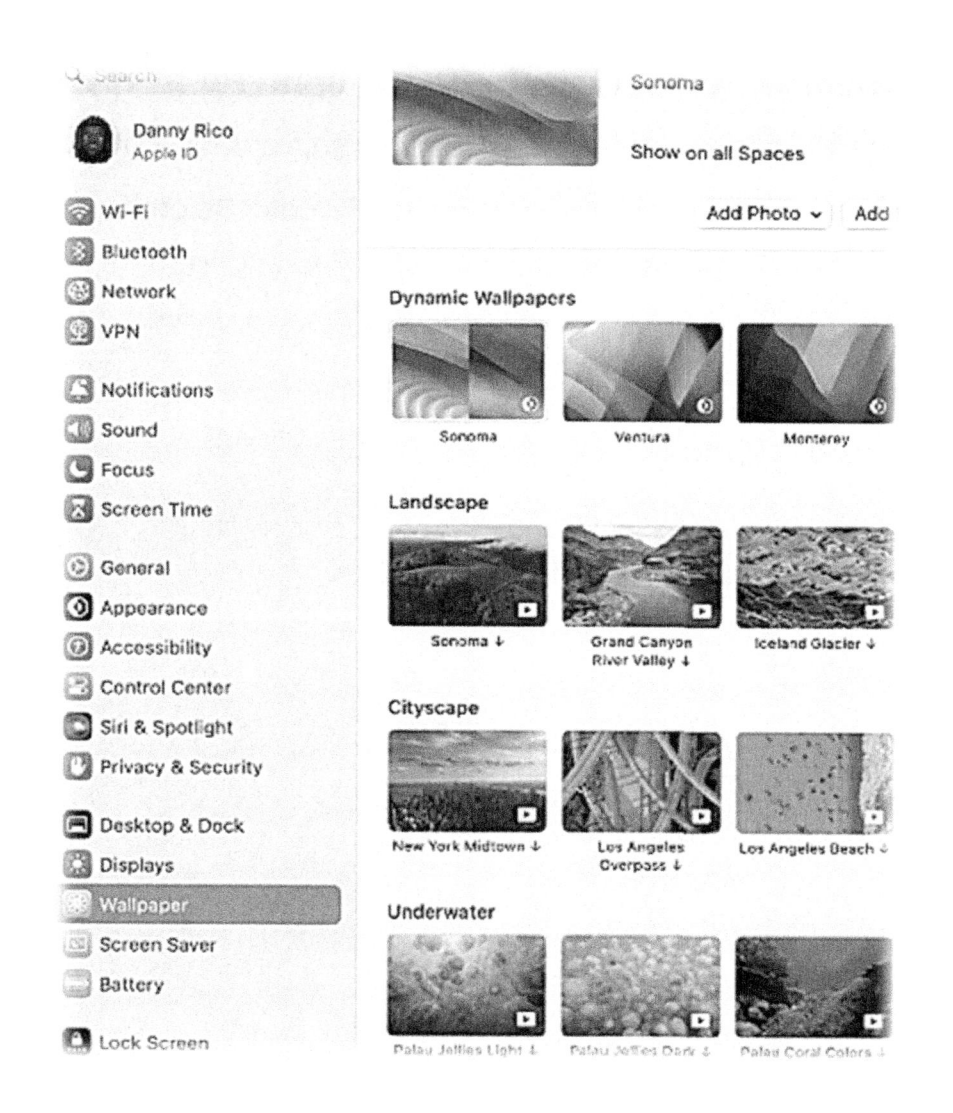

Change the wallpaper or background color of your computer: To have your desktop photographs and colors rotate automatically, click the Auto-Rotate icon next to a custom folder or color. The buttons at the very top of Wallpaper settings allow you to choose a certain time interval or select a cycle pattern at random.

Choose an item from the floating menu at the top of Wallpaper settings to rearrange or resize your desktop image. Fill Screen, Fit to Screen, Stretch to Fill Screen, Center, and others are just a few of the available options.

CHAPTER 4

Pin Notes

- Right-clicking a note and selecting "Pin Note" will do the trick.
- Now it will appear beside the pinned symbol at the very top of the display.
- If you change your mind and want to unpin it, just right-click it and choose "Unpin Note."

Float Notes

- Choose a note to float it. Then, press the Window menu and pick float Selected Note.

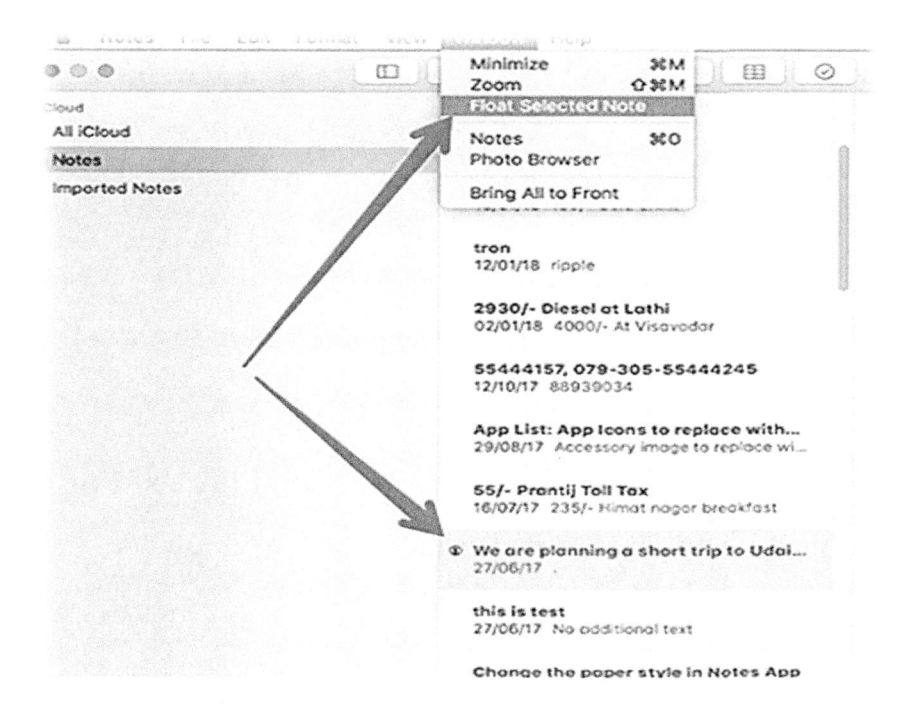

How to import files to Notes

- On the Notes app, choose Import from the File menu.
- Choose the file and hit the Import icon.

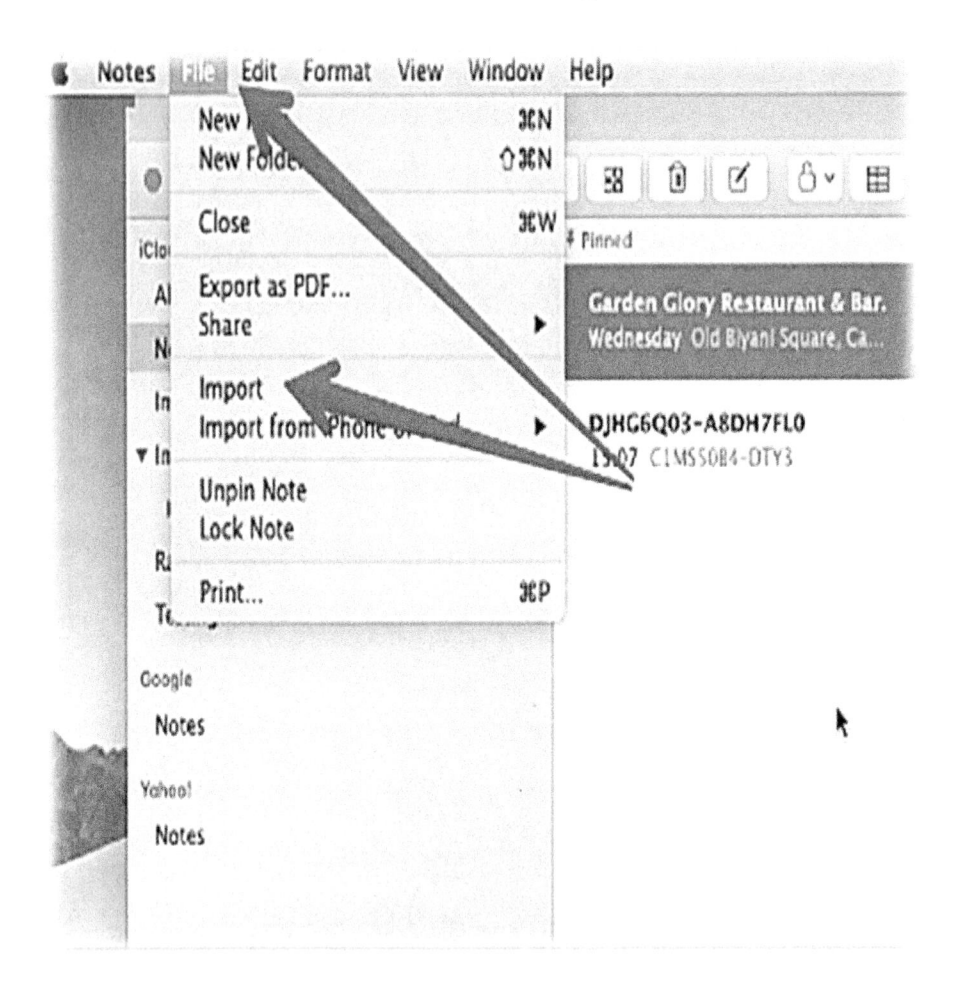

- To finish, choose Import Notes and hit the Confirm icon. The note will be imported and placed in the appropriate area.

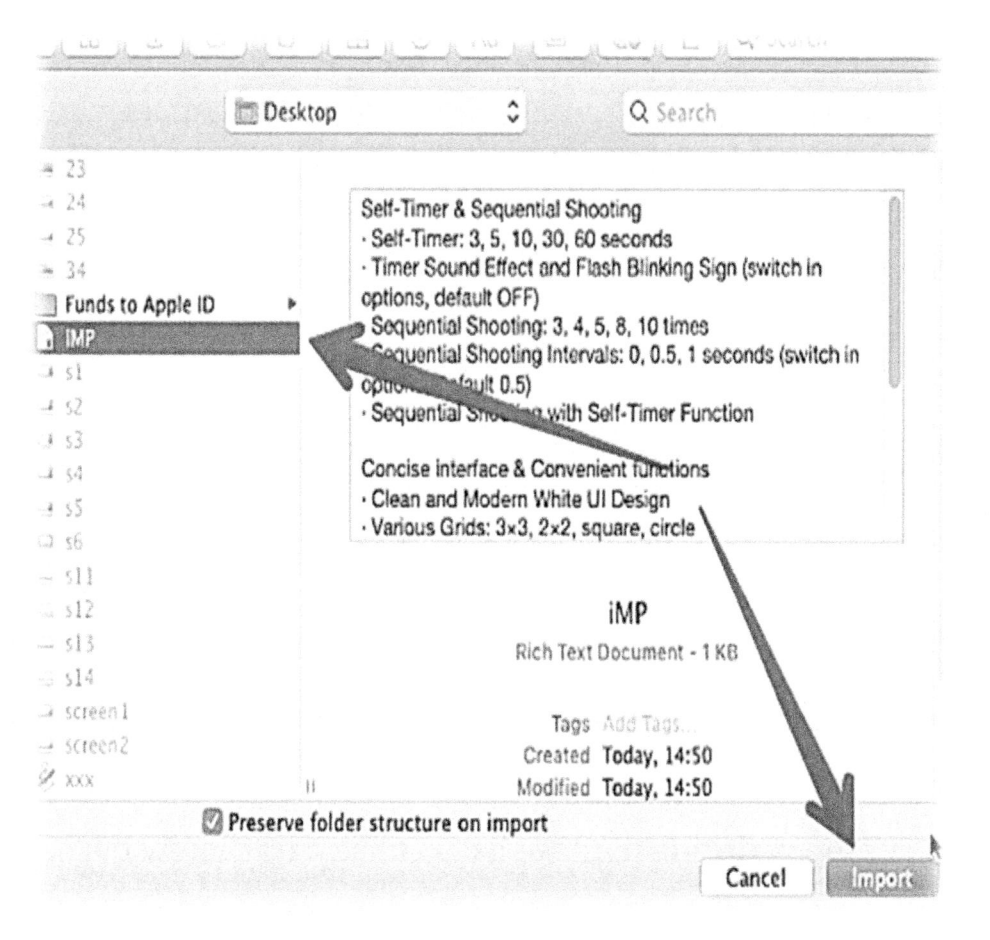

How to export Notes as PDF

After writing a lengthy memo, you can choose to turn it into a portable PDF for easier sharing.

- Go to the File menu and choose Export Note.
- Then, give it a title, tag it appropriately, and decide where you want it to go. When you are finished, click the Save icon.

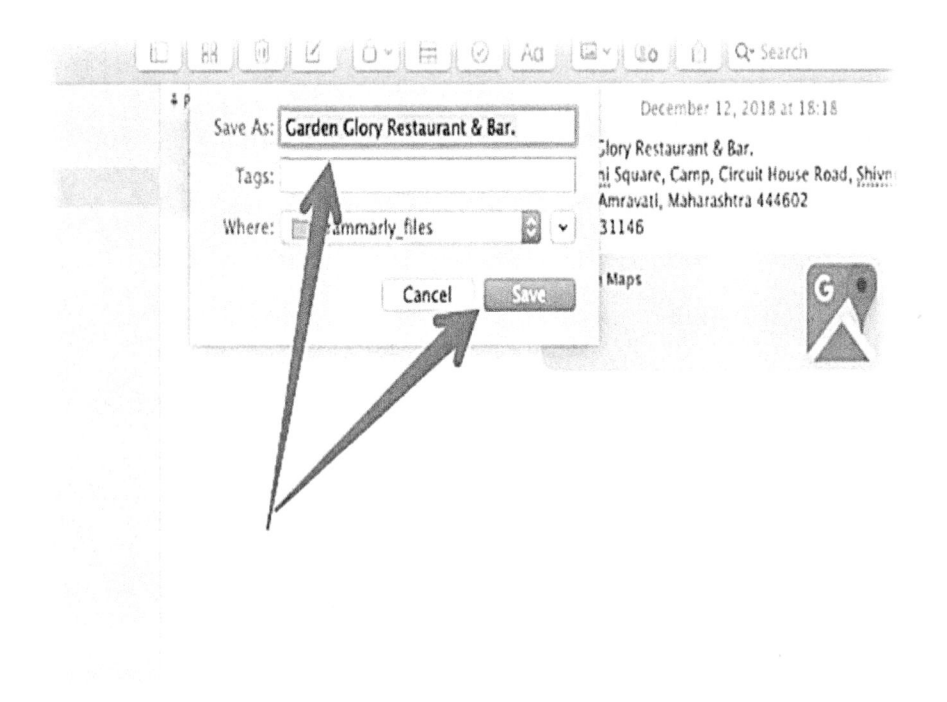

Note Checklist

- If you decide to make a checklist, carry on by putting the mouse in before the first item and then clicking the "Make a checklist icon." Proceed by typing in the names of all the items now.

Include Tables to Notes

Including tables in a note just takes a single click. Literally.

- Select the small tables icon to create a comprehensive spreadsheet for the scheduled meetings. Instantly, a table will be included.

- Next, add a row or column before or after your current one by right-clicking the little Add Row/Column icon.

```
/* Style Sheet Last updated - 2/18/200

/* Heading 9, procedure Heading,lproch */
.lproch         {font-size: 110%; font-weight: bold; margin-top: 1.2em; }

/* Paragraph class styles */

.ac             {font-size: smaller; }
.alpha          {font-size: 110%; font-weight: bold; color: #000088; }
.dt1            {text-indent: 2em; margin-left: 2em;}
.hang           {text-indent: -2em; margin-left: 2em;}
.fixp           {color: #00ff00 /* fix this paragraph for incorrectly used styles / green */
.ind            {margin-left: 2em;}
.ind2           {margin-left: 4em;}
.l1             {font-size: 95%; font-weight: bold; }
.l2             {font-size: 95%; margin-left: 2em; }
.l3             {font-size: 95%; margin-left: 4em; }
.minionly       {background-color: #FFD7F9; }
.mt             {margin-top: 2em; font-weight: bold;}
.note{
    font-size: 11px;
    color: #000088;
}
```

52

Sort Notes

- To do this, launch the app, go to the Notes menu, choose Preferences, and then select the desired choice from the Sort notes by drop-down menu.

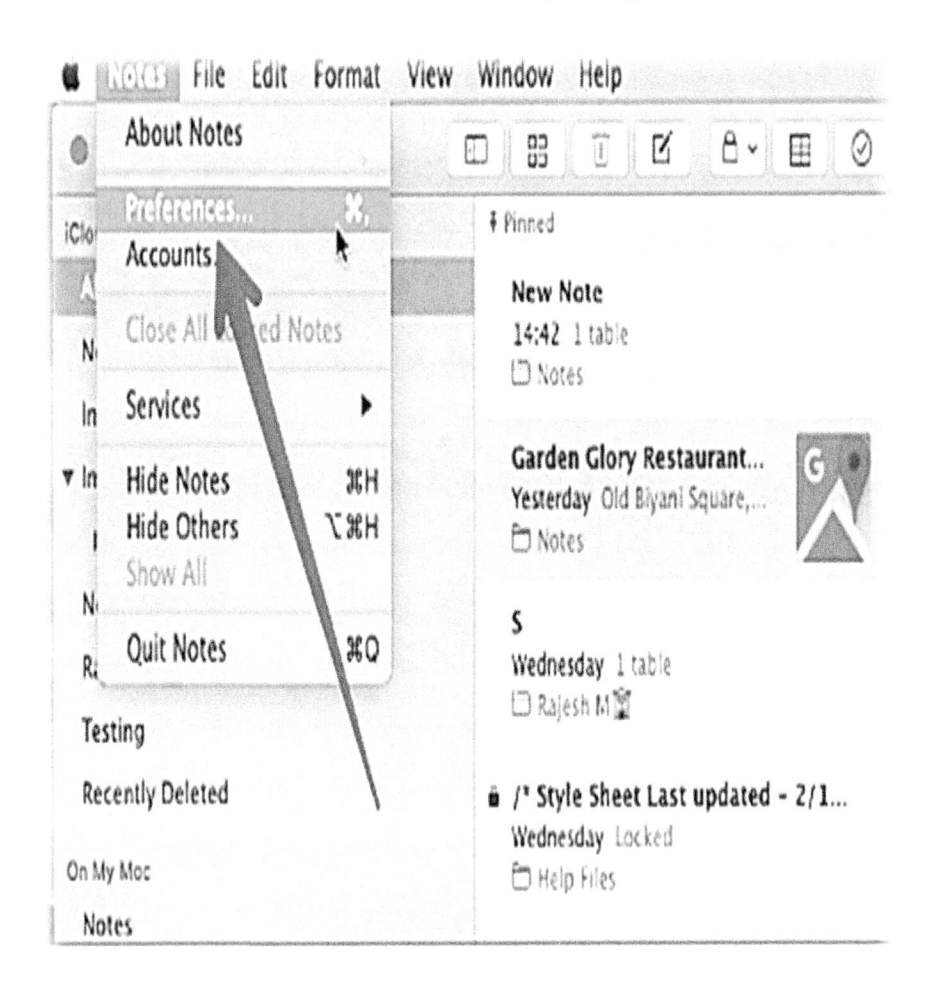

Collaborate with Notes

- Launch the note, click the People icon, choose the appropriate medium, and then share it.

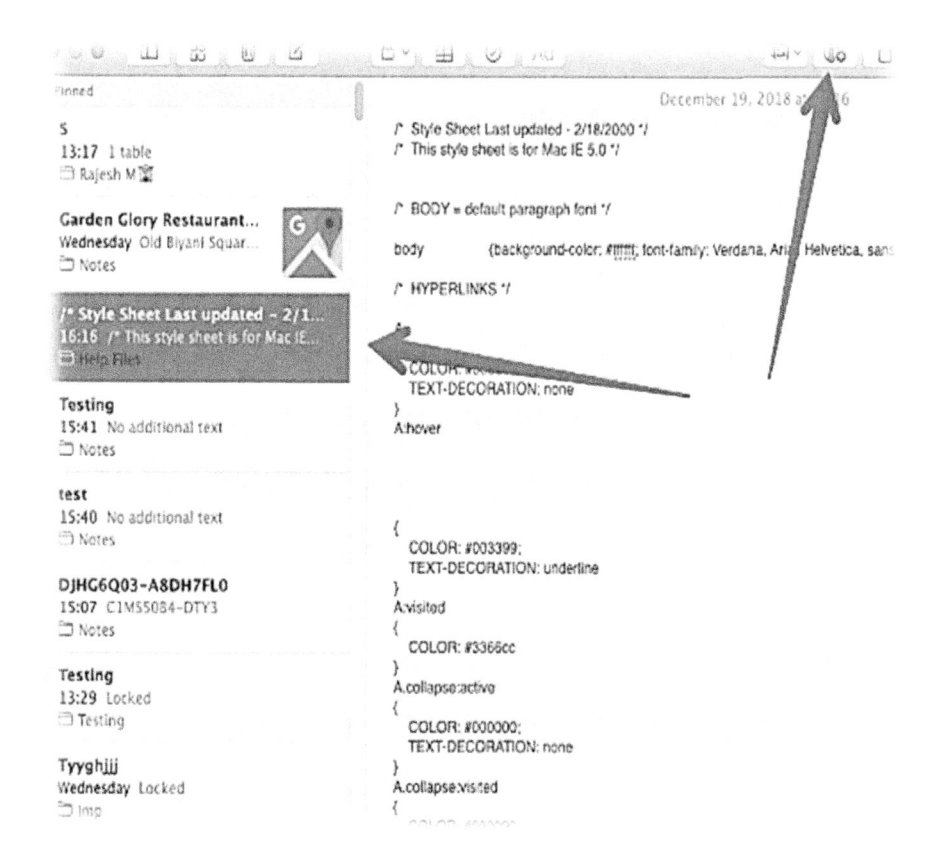

Apple Note Tags

- To assign a tag to a note, just write the hash symbol (#) and the word or words you wish to use.
- Using the #diet tag, you can easily sort through all of your Notes to find the ones that pertain to your diet plan for the week.
- If you click a tag in the Tags sidebar, all of your notes that include that tag will be shown. All the notes that have that tag will be shown.

Lock Notes

You can lock a note in two ways:

- Enter File > Lock Note via menu or press the Padlock icon on the toolbar.

Notes will then prompt you to set a password and a hint. Once a password is established, it must be entered whenever the note is accessed or modified.

CHAPTER 5

Start Siri with "Siri"

Siri was previously activated on macOS by either clicking the Siri menu bar icon or saying "Hey Siri." However, with the new version, you can just say "Siri" to launch it, making the process much more natural and unobtrusive.

Set up an iCloud Account

- Click "System Preferences" > "Apple ID" from the Apple menu.
- Press create Apple ID.

- Type in your birth year and then press the Next icon.
- First, you'll need to input your name, email address, and password. Click Get a free iCloud email account if you don't want to use your existing email address.
- To finish the creation, just stick to the on-display directions.

Your new iCloud account should be activated as soon as you establish your Apple ID and pass the verification process in macOS. The option to combine your calendar and contact lists will be presented to you at some point.

Do you want to merge Contacts, Calendars, Safari, News and Stocks with iCloud?

Your information on this Mac will be uploaded and merged with the Contacts, Calendars, Safari, News and Stocks stored in iCloud.

Don't Merge   Merge

- Select Merge to begin syncing the specified data. Click Don't Merge if you'd rather make your selections separately, then proceed with the setup as usual.
- When asked, choose Allow to activate Find My Mac.

View iCloud Space

- Open settings.
- By selecting your name, you will be sent to your Apple ID profile.
- Select iCloud to see your total iCloud space.
- To get an app-by-app analysis of storage use, choose Manage Storage.

The same steps apply when using a Mac to access your storage in System Preferences. The preceding images should serve as a reminder that if your iCloud storage is at 100%, you either need more space or a better plan. From the iCloud Storage display, you can get right into things by clicking Upgrade.

How Do I Set a limit on iCloud Storage

- Open settings.
- By selecting your name, you will enter your Apple ID profile.

- Select "iCloud".
- To disable an app, just slide the toggle switch. The "on" setting grants iCloud access to all applications.
- Save data locally by choosing Keep on My iPhone. Pick remove on My iPhone to delete data.

Free Up iCloud Storage space

If you need to make some room in iCloud but have run out of space, you should first determine what content is taking up the most space.

- Navigate to [Your Name] > iCloud > Manage Storage on your iPhone's Settings menu.
- If you need to manage your iCloud account, choose System Preferences > Apple ID > iCloud, then click Manage from your Mac's Apple menu.

What is using up space on your iCloud account can be seen here. Photos, chats, backups, iCloud Drive, and applications are the frequent common instances. How to make room for each of them is detailed below.

Remove iCloud Backups That Aren't Needed

- Enter Settings, pick your name > "iCloud," then "Manage Storage," then "Backups".

- The backed-up devices list will now appear. After selecting a device, choose Delete Backup > Turn Off & Delete. This action will delete the selected iCloud backup.
- You can also see the backup of devices you're currently using to disable app data saving to iCloud. The program in question attempted to add 600 MB of data to our iCloud backup, despite the fact that we seldom use it.

To disable this behavior, choose Show All Apps from the device menu. Turn off app-specific backups and delete them with the push of a button. By doing so, the corresponding app data will be excluded from future iCloud backups.

Select System Preferences > Apple ID > iCloud from the Apple menu on a Mac. To access backups, go to Manage > Backups. Selective deletion of backups is now an option.

Remove old Messages

Follow these instructions to swiftly free up space on iCloud if the Messages app is hogging all your storage.

- Navigate to your device's Settings menu, then tap Messages.
- Next, press the Delete icon after lowering the Keep Messages setting from Forever to 30 days or a year. Messages that are more than a month or a year old will be deleted automatically.

Messages can quickly accumulate and take up too much space in your iCloud account, but this is a simple fix.

- Then, let's get rid of some of these crowded conversations. To access Messages, go to Settings > [Your Name] > iCloud > Manage Storage > Messages. Next, choose Recent Topics.
- This will let you see which conversations are eating up your iCloud storage capacity.
- You can remove unwanted conversations by tapping Edit in the upper right corner and then marking them. The conversation can then be erased by tapping the trash can symbol in the conversation's upper right edge.

Delete individual messages instead of the whole thread by tapping the conversation in the list. To see a contact's photos, press the contact's name at the top, then tap Info.

If you tap See All, you'll be able to manually remove any unwanted media. You can also delete huge attachments in a conversation by going to the Documents tab.

Use Universal Control between Macs

Using Universal Control, you can pair your Mac with a nearby device and operate both with a single set of input devices (keyboard, mouse, trackpad).

Keep in mind that you can have to re-establish the connection with Universal Control if you don't use it for a while.

- Pick one of the options below:
1. Move the cursor to the far right or far left of the Mac screen using the mouse or trackpad. If a border pops up on your Mac's display, just drag your cursor beyond it to continue navigating.
2. Select System Preferences from the Apple menu, and then click Displays in the left pane. Please scroll down if necessary. Select a device to link your keyboard and mouse to by clicking the corresponding button under "Add Display" on the right. Move the cursor from Mac's screen and onto the other device using a mouse or trackpad.

3. In the Mac menu bar, choose Control Center, then click Display, and finally, select a device under "Link keyboard and mouse to." Move the cursor from the Mac's display and onto the other device using a mouse or trackpad.

Which side of the display you connect your devices to depends on the direction in which you shift the pointer while doing so. You can modify this behavior by reshuffling your devices in the Displays preferences. You can reposition the display by pressing and dragging its picture.

Your Mac can be configured to instantly link up with any other Mac or iPad in range.

Select System Preferences from the Apple menu, then click Displays on the left. Please scroll down if necessary. In the right-hand menu, under "Advanced," choose "Automatically reconnect to any nearby Mac or iPad."

Disconnect Mac from other gadgets

- Select System settings from the Apple menu, and then tap Displays in the sidebar. Scroll down if necessary.
- To disconnect, choose your display on the right.

Disable Universal Control

If you don't want your Mac to be able to recognize external keyboards and mice or trackpads, you can disable Universal Control.

- Select System Preferences in the Apple menu, and then hit Displays in the left pane. Please scroll down if necessary.
- Choose one of the following after clicking the Advanced icon on the right:

Disconnect all Universal Control: Disable "allows your pointer and keyboard to shift between any nearby Mac or iPad."

Keep the mouse from making contact when it reaches the screen's border: Remove the checkmark from "Push through the edge of a display to link to a nearby Mac or iPad."

Organize desktop Manually

The desktop is one of the first places you can start cleaning up on your Mac. It's a good idea to clean it up if it's packed with outdated documents and folders. Several options exist for manual desktop organization:

- Examine every file and folder sitting on your Mac's desktop, then move the ones that don't belong there to more appropriate locations (such as the Documents folder).
- Making a fresh folder and putting all the previous files and folders in it is a simple way to tidy up your desktop. Use a label like "old desktop data" to describe it.

Desktop Stacks

- Right-click On any part of the desktop and press Use Stacks.

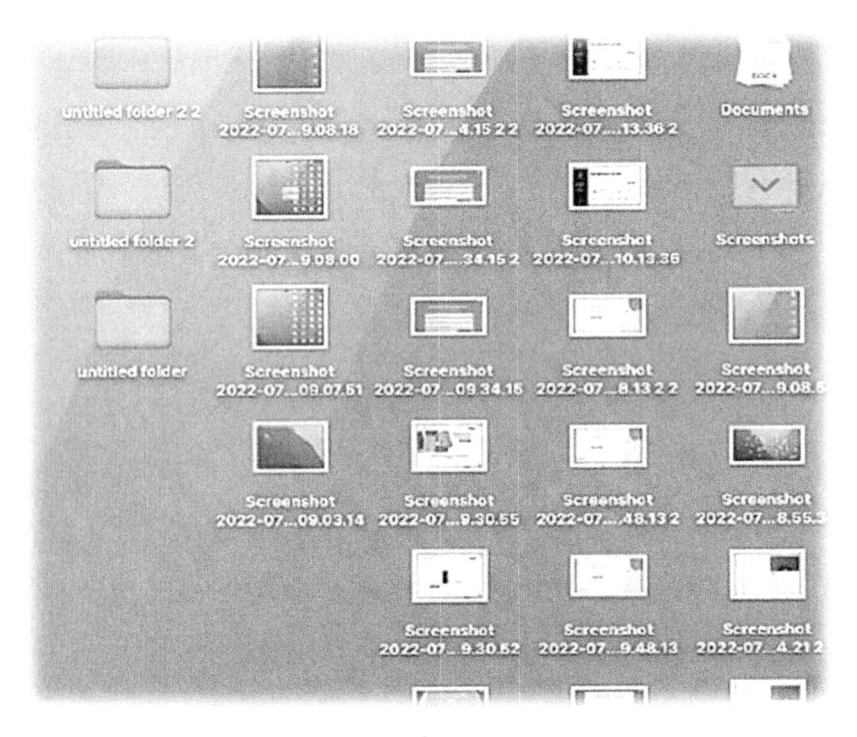

- Your disorganized files will be neatly organized by macOS.
- You can see the contents of any of these folders by clicking on the corresponding tab.
- To dismiss a Stack, just click its name.

CHAPTER 6

Spring-loaded folders

To be sure, "spring-loaded folders" are excellent at one thing and nothing else. On a Mac, if you hold down the command key and drag an item to a folder, the folder will open and you can continue dragging inside it.

Or to a subfolder of the original folder. That spring opens, giving you access to even deeper levels of folder nesting. As soon as you release the item you're dragging, the folders snap shut again before you can decide whether you actually need that many.

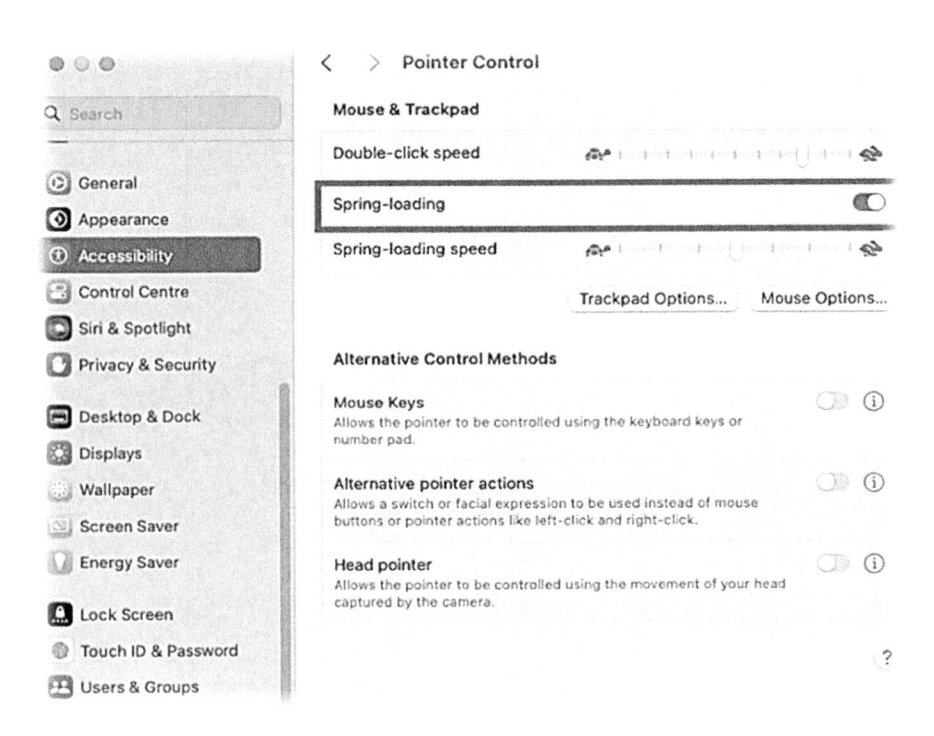

Activate and deactivate spring-loaded folders

- Launch System settings.
- Select accessibility.
- Move down then Pick Pointer Control.
- Press to switch on and off Spring loading.

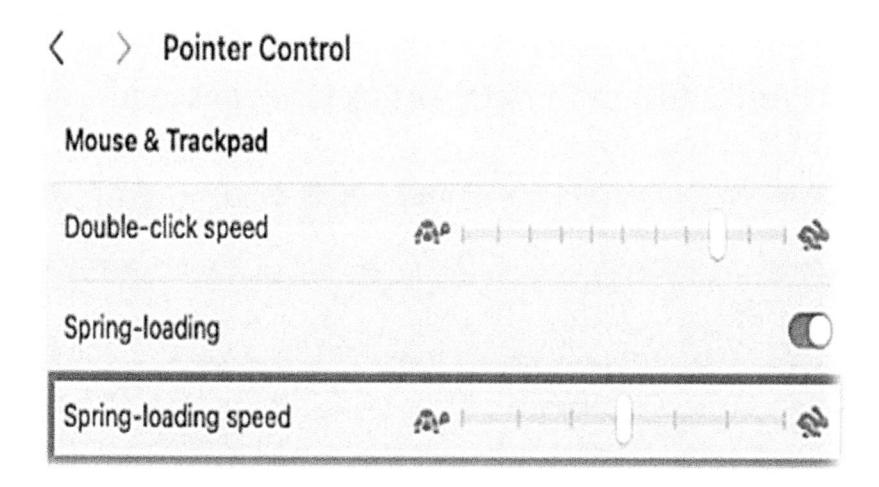

Make spring-loaded folders quicker or slower

Changing the speed to something more suitable for your requirements is preferable to turning off the function entirely. The spring-loaded folders are activated and set at a moderate pace by default.

- To eliminate any lag, move the speed slid to its far rightmost position. The speed is so great that the files no longer "spring open;" rather, they move from closed to open in a single moment.

Also, if you move the slider to its minimal position on the left, you can count to four before the folder automatically opens.

Organize Important folders in the sidebar

- Locate the folder where you'd want to place the shortcut.
- Press and shift it to Favorites in Finder's sidebar.

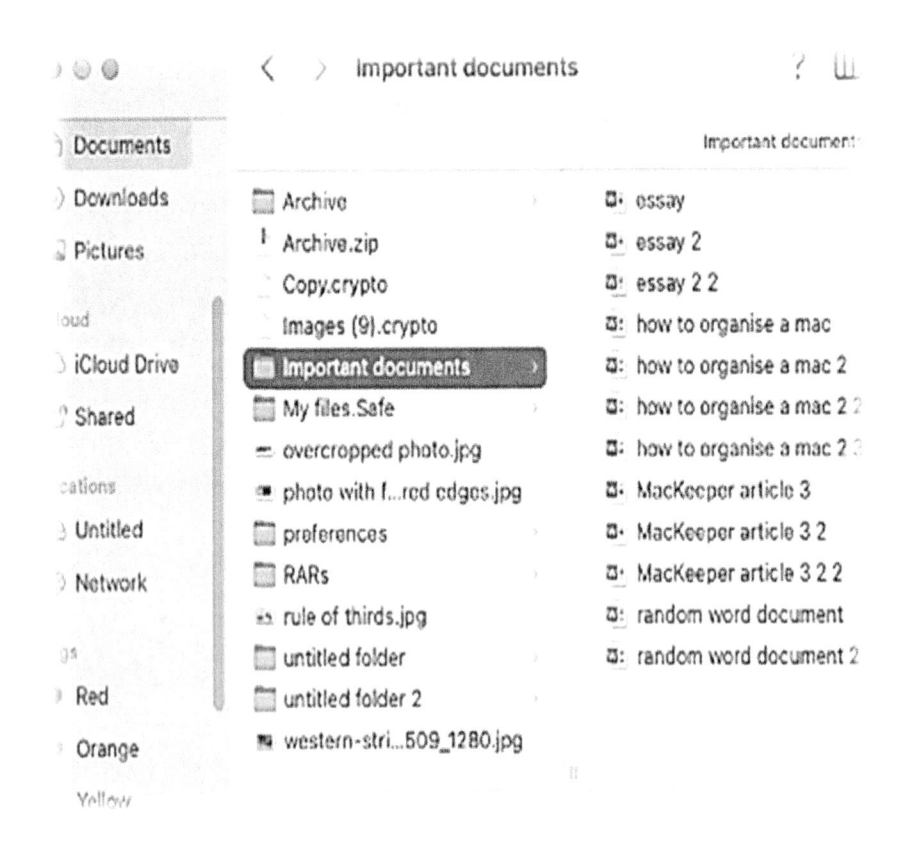

- Third, release the mouse button when a horizontal line appears.

Use tags to organize files and folder

The original folder can be accessed at any time by selecting this new link.

- Right-clicking a file or folder and choosing a predefined tag color is the quickest way to utilize tags.
- Alternatively, you can choose a color by clicking the tag icon in Finder.

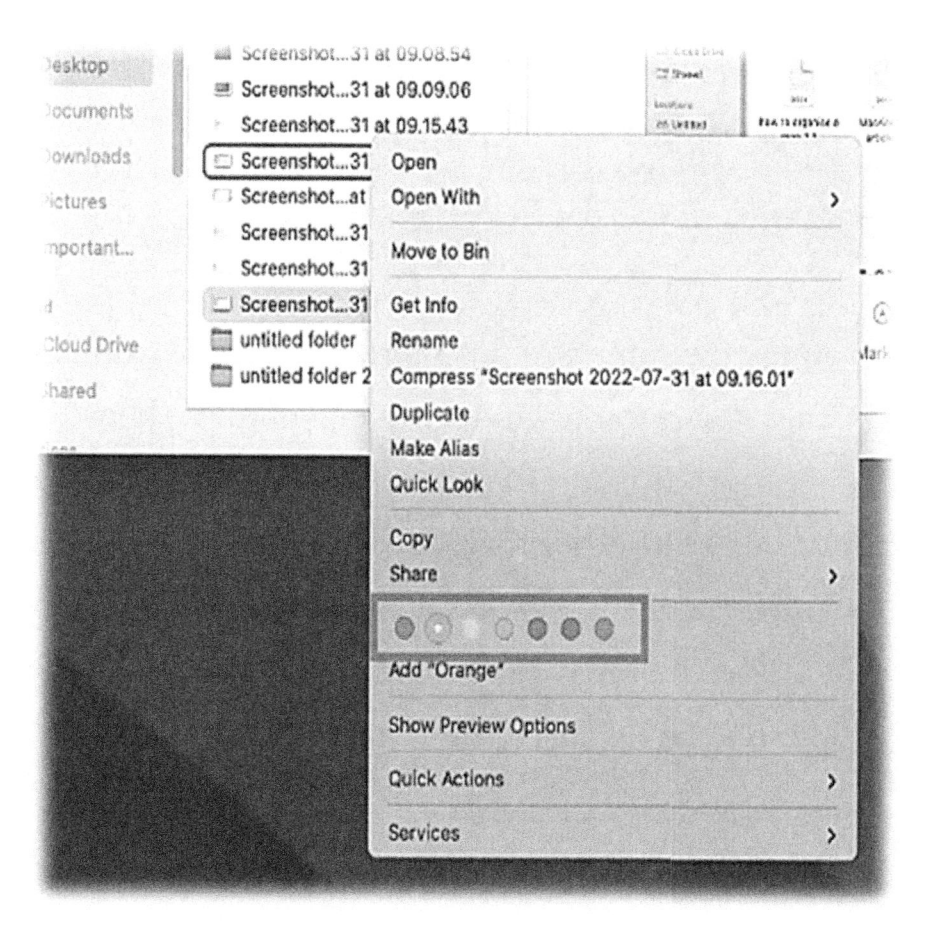

- Third, a colorful dot will appear next to the item you've marked.

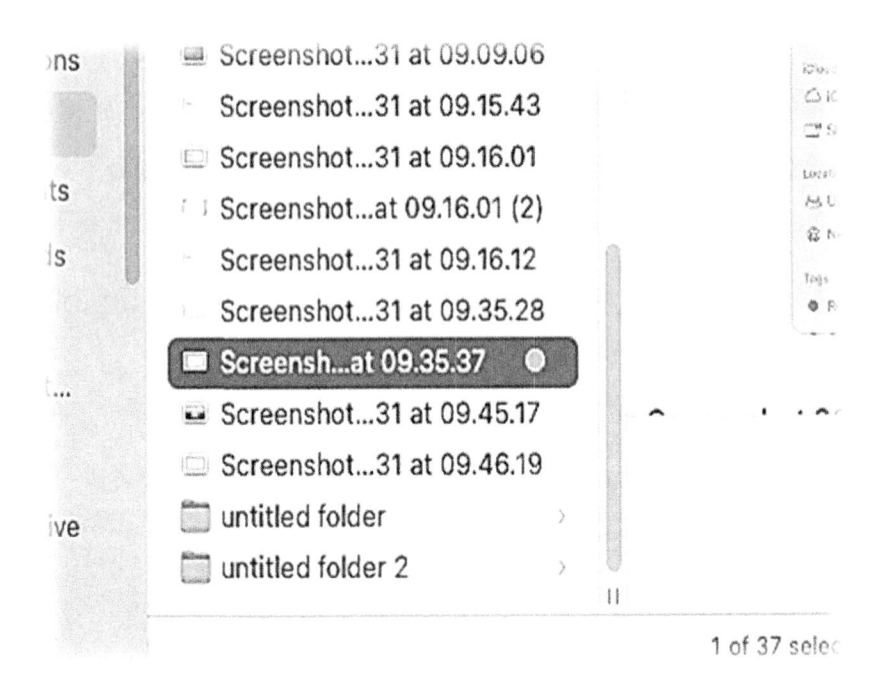

- Apply the same to a few more items, then launch the Tags list in the Finder's sidebar and choose the appropriate color. Items with the same color tags will be shown together.
- You have the option of making your own tags. Access the Tags menu by right-clicking a file.
- Input a name, pick a color, and hit enter

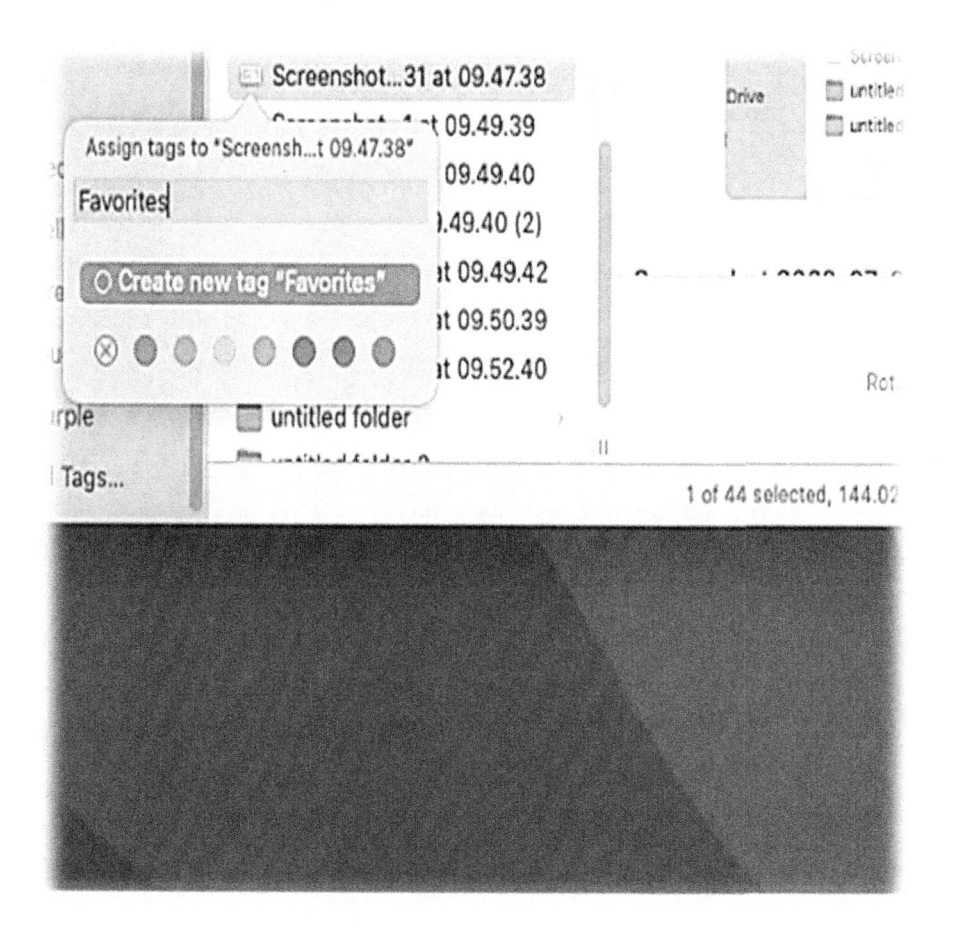

- Finder > Preferences > Tags is where you'll make any more changes.

Use decluttering tools

- Go to Apple > About This Mac from the menu bar.
- Next, choose Manage from the Storage tab.
- Below Reduce Clutter in the recommendation section, select Review Files.

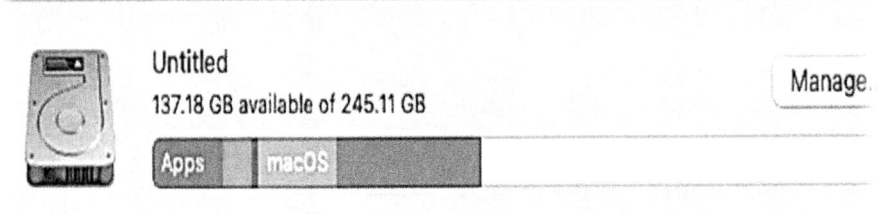

- Handle Archive > Suggestions > File Evaluation.
- Here is where you can search for and delete things like large files, downloads, apps that aren't supported, and more.

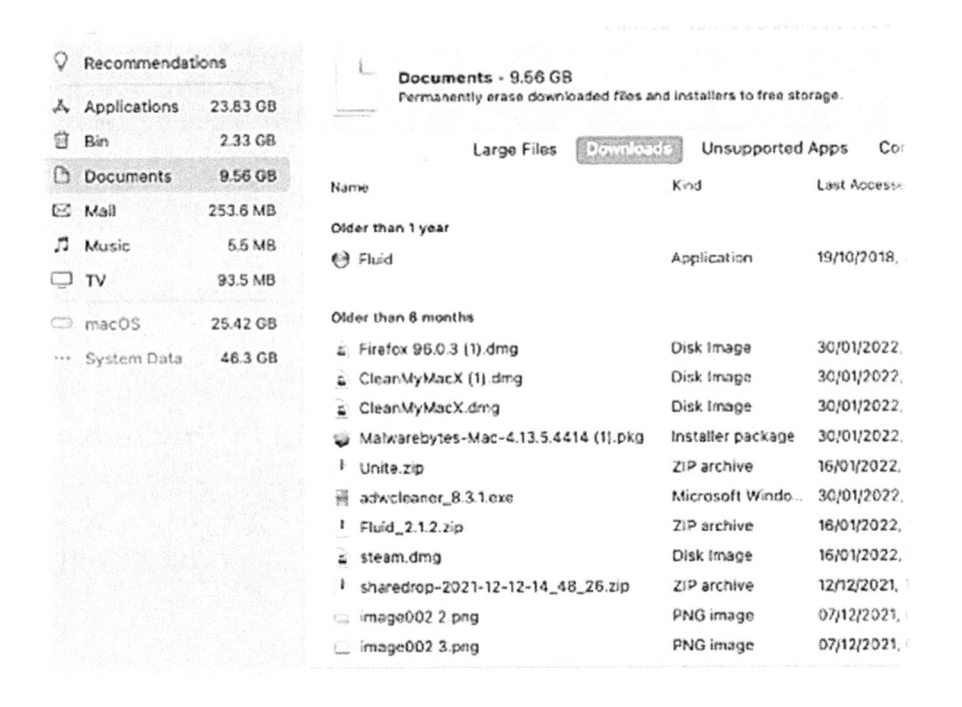

Delete duplicate Files

- Go to the "Duplicates Finder" section of MacKeeper, and then click "Start scan."
- Hold tight until the scan is finished.

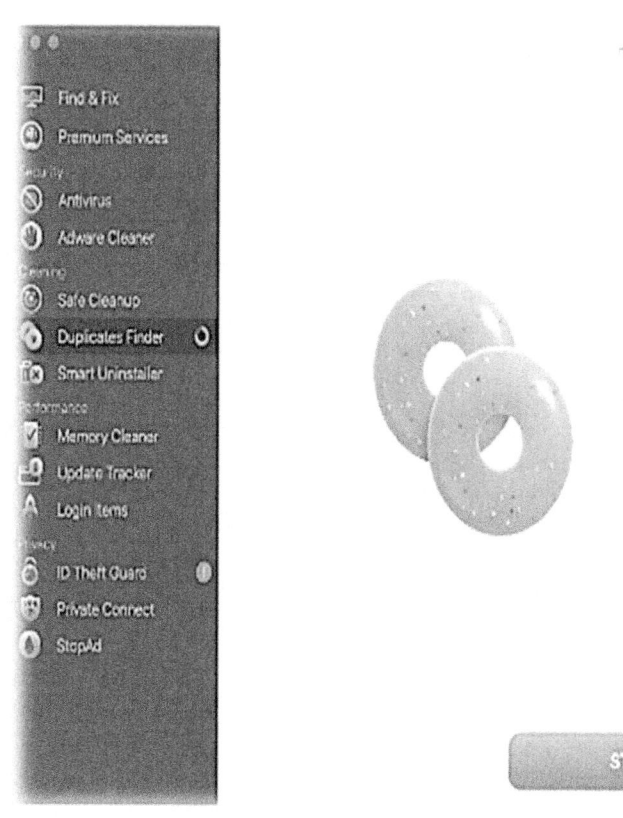

- Third, MacKeeper will give you the option to choose Duplicates, Similar Photos, and Screenshots after it's done. To delete all of them at once, just pick them and click the Remove Selected icon.

- You can also see further information by clicking on the individual headings. One-by-one deletions can be made from that menu.

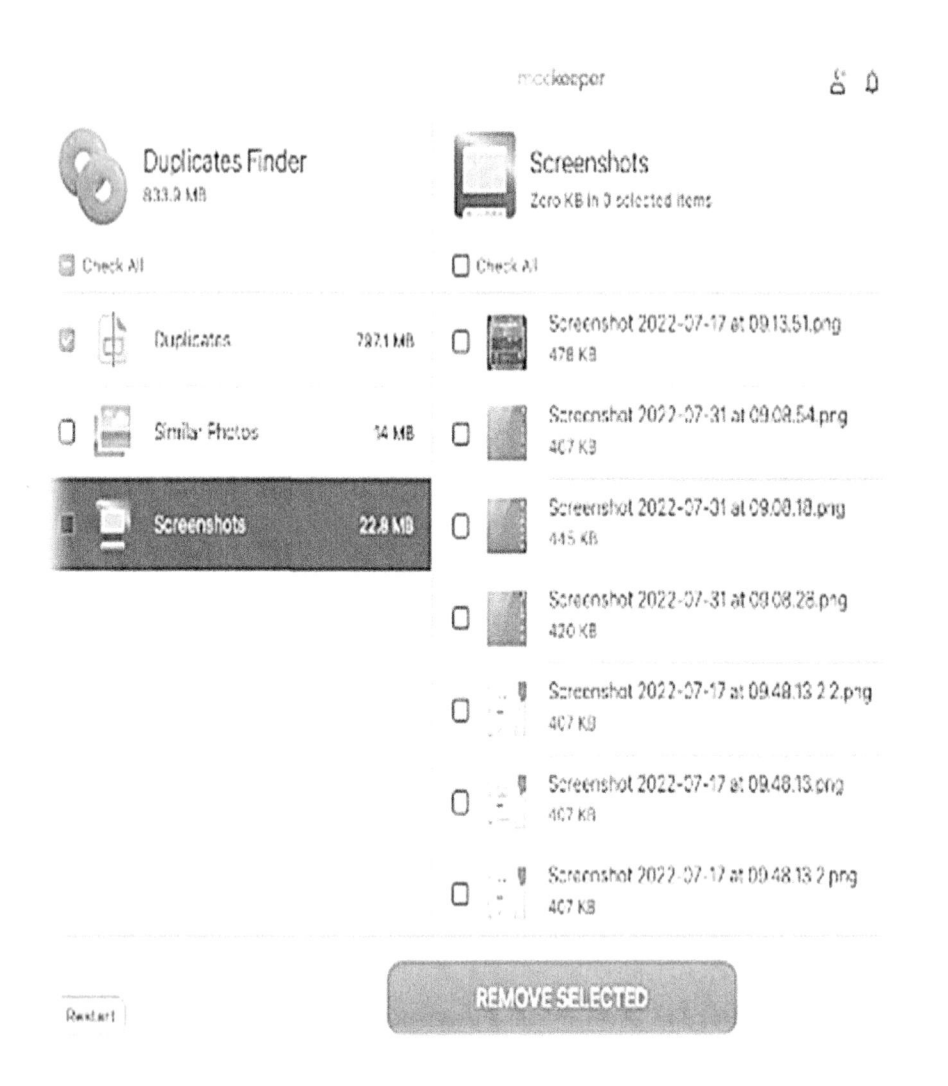

Use Smart Folders to group files

- To make a new Smart Folder in Finder, go to File > press New Smart Folder.

- Here you can limit your search to the current location or use This Mac to search everything.

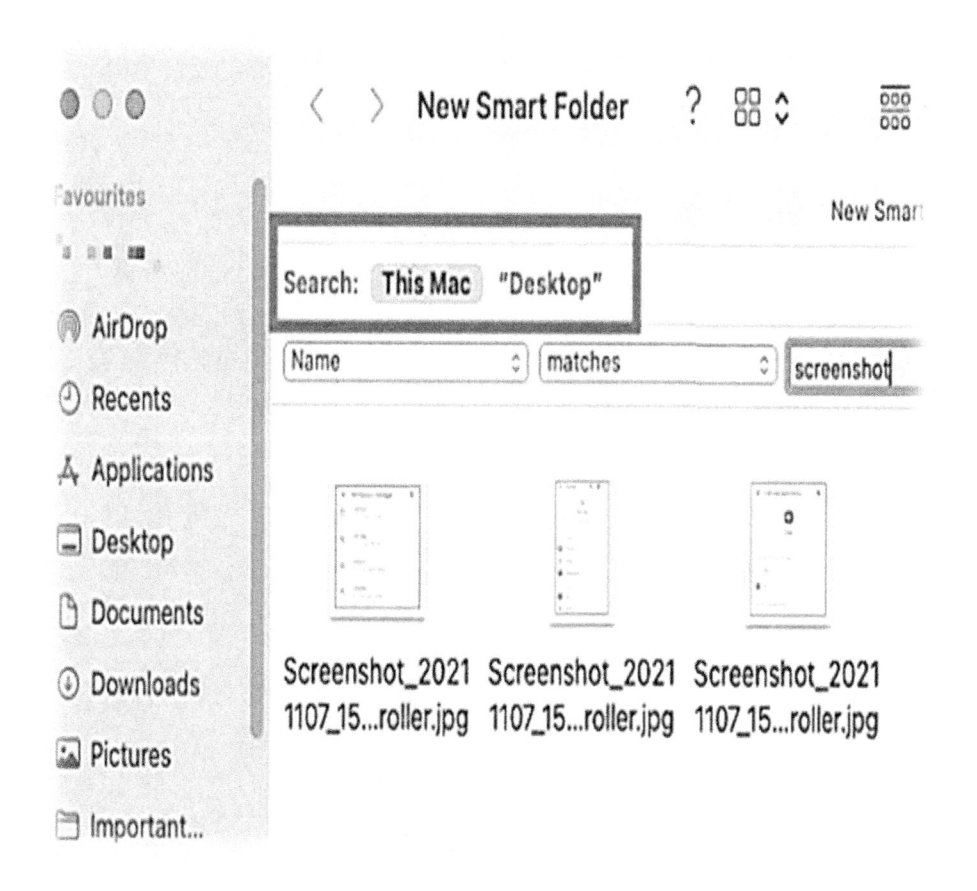

- Expand your search by pressing the plus sign.
- Select attributes like Type, Title, and Date Created from the respective pull-down options.
- Additional filtering choices become available when you choose Other.

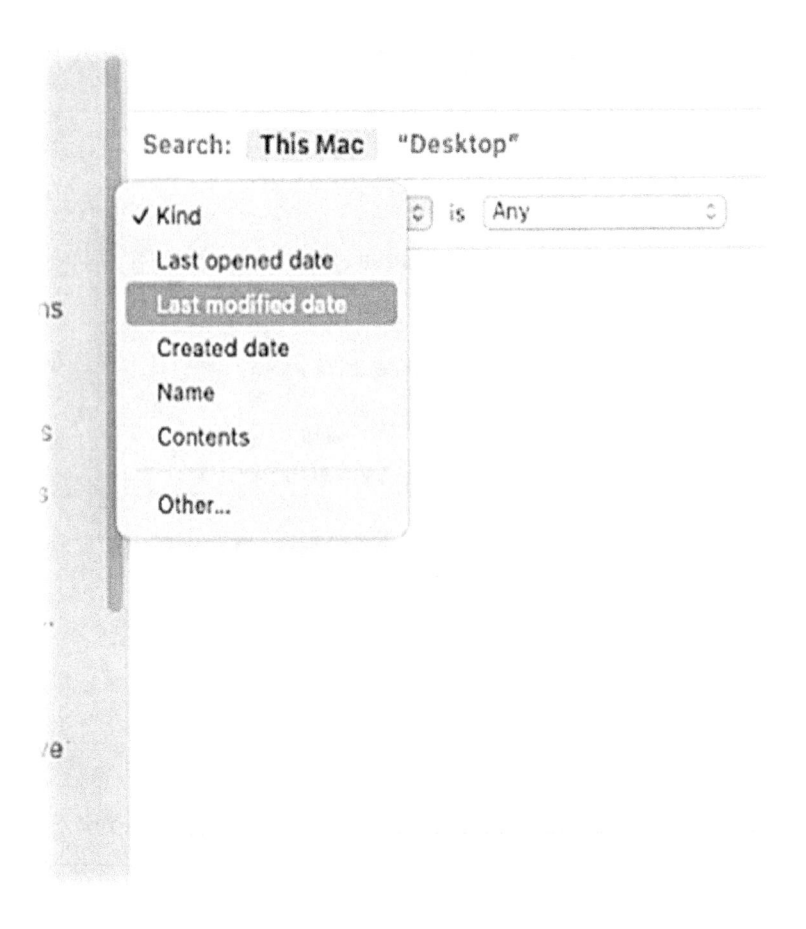

- Add more filters as needed, then click "Save"
- Designate a place and a name for your Smart Folder. You have the option of including it in the Finder's sidebar. Finalize by selecting the Save option.
- From now on, your Smart Folder will be updated automatically anytime a new file is created that matches your search parameters.

Set a folder's view

- To launch a new Finder window on your Mac, choose the Finder icon from the Dock.
- Choose a folder, either one already present in the Finder's sidebar like Recents or Desktop or one you've created.

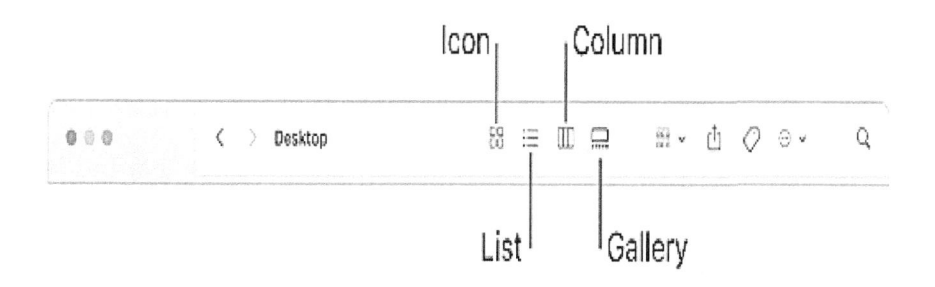

Icon Column

List Gallery

- To see the View options in a row or expand the window size, press the View icon in the Finder's toolbar.

How to customize folder View

In Icon view, for instance, you can alter the grid spacing and size of the icon to better suit your needs. You can also make this view your default for this and all other folders.

- To launch a new Finder window on your Mac, choose the Finder icon from the Dock.

- Pick View > press Show View Options or press Command-J, then choose the folder you prefer to modify.
- Adjust the settings to see just the files in the current folder the way you like.

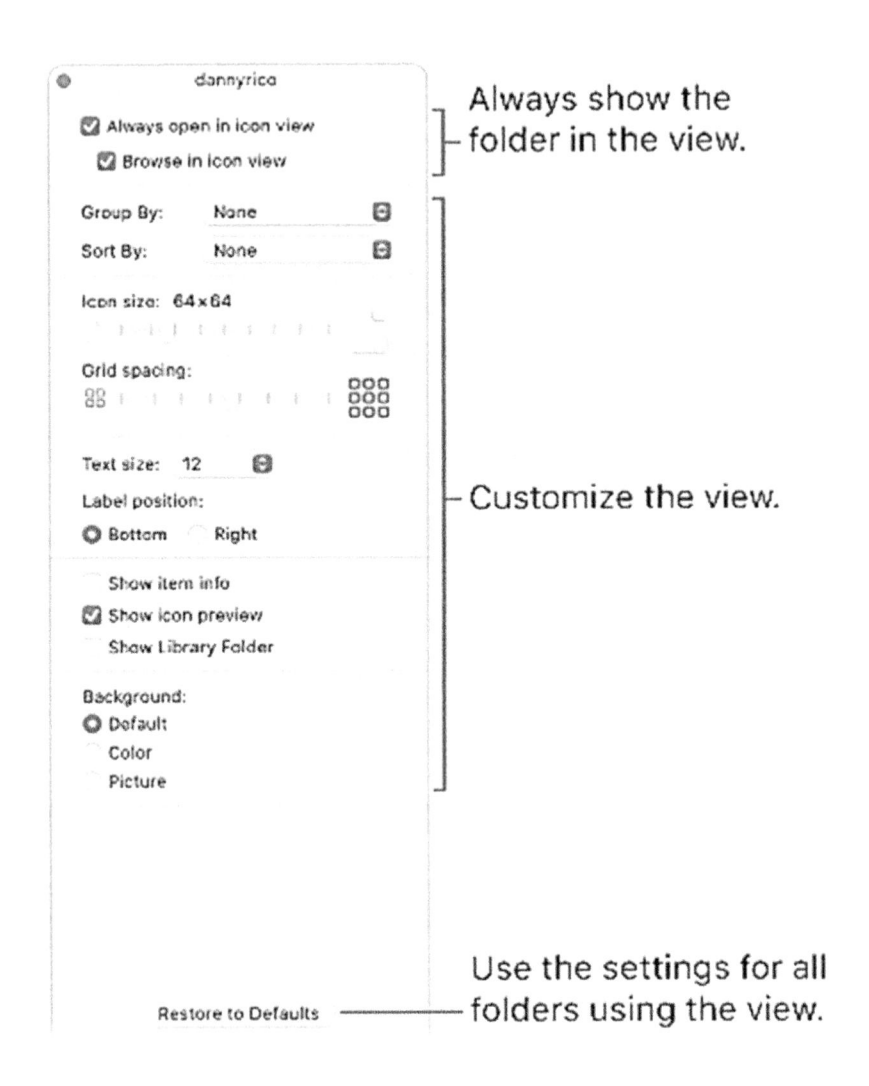

Always show the folder in the view.

Customize the view.

Use the settings for all folders using the view.

Options vary among views. You can customize the presentation of current dates in List view and conceal filenames in Gallery view, for instance.

- Select whether this view should be used permanently for this and other folders.
- Close the options window after you're done with it by clicking Close or pressing Command-J.

CHAPTER 7

Share internet

The internet connection on your Mac can easily be converted into a Wi-Fi hotspot with only a few adjustments.

- To begin, open the Sharing preferences, click sharing, and tick the box for Internet Sharing. When prompted, choose the Start icon.
- Switch on Personal Hotspot under Settings > Cellular on your iPhone. After that, your Mac will recognize your mobile device as a network option.

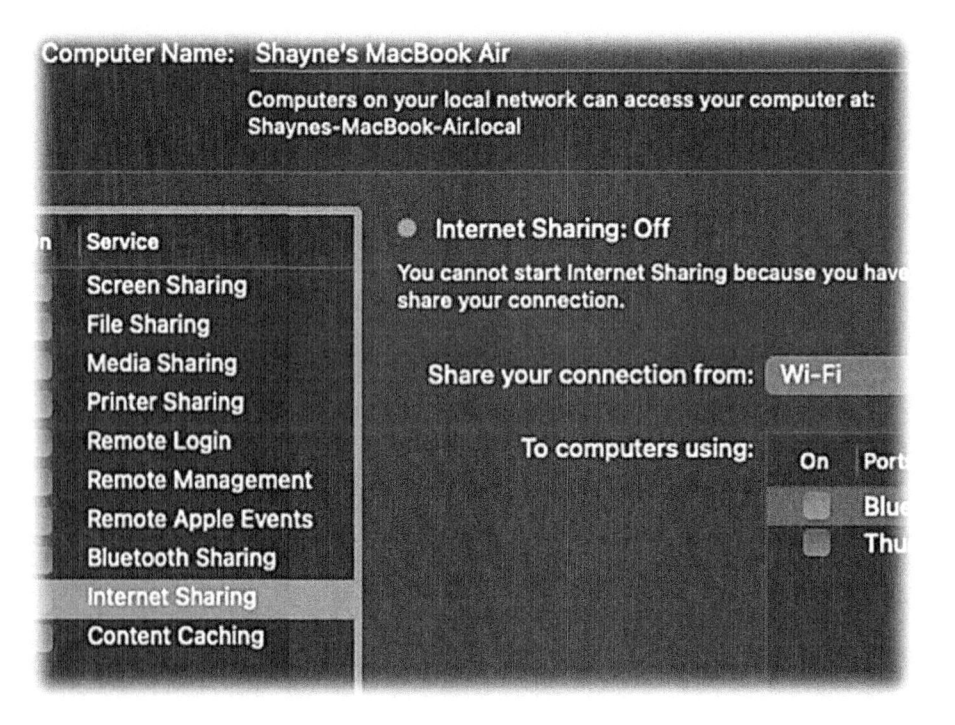

Create Memoji

- System Preferences > Users and Groups is where you'll find your user profile image.

Be sure your user profile is chosen in the left column of the Users and Groups option, and then tap on your photo in the right column.

- When you open the selection window, Memoji will be listed in the first column on the left. To the right, you'll find options to get individual emoji or make your own Memoji.

- Simply hit the "+" icon to create a brand new Memoji. From the skin to the clothes, you'll learn about every aspect of making a Memoji.

And your Memoji is always open to customization, and you can make new ones anytime you choose.

- When you're through customizing your Memoji, choose the icon that says "Done" at the edge to the right.
- Return to the selector box after making your Memoji, and choose it as your user photo. You can choose the backdrop color and even posture it in a unique way.
- To zoom in or out, use the slider that's located in the left column, just below your image.
- When you've finished customizing your Memoji to your liking, just hit the "Save" icon. When next you log in to your Mac, your Memoji will appear on the login screen.

How to create a personal voice

- Enter System Settings, and press Accessibility in the left sidebar.
- Select "Personal Voice" under the Speech heading in the main window's main section.
- The personal voice segment will be displayed. Select the option for Make a personal voice.
- Prepare to be recorded.

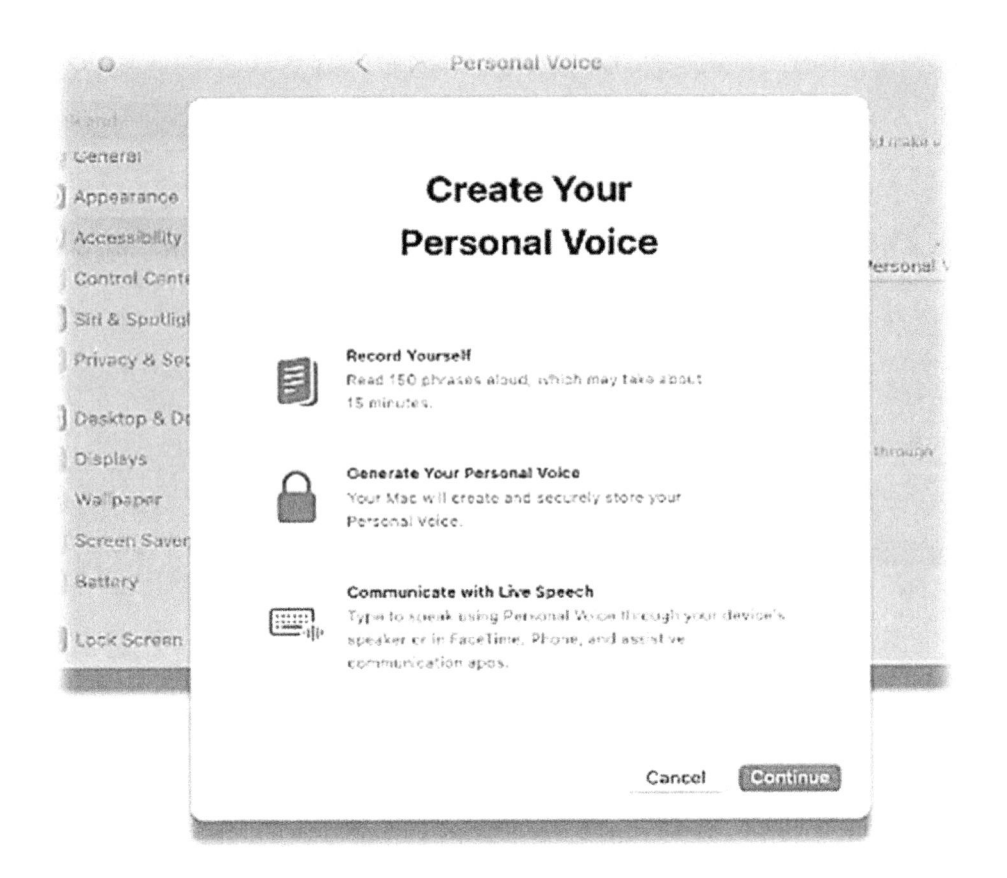

A welcome message is shown once the user enters their password. You'll need to memorize 150 sentences to utilize in your Personal Voice, it says. This voice can then be utilized in applications like FaceTime and Phone. It takes around 15–20 minutes to complete. If you want to proceed, please do so.

A second welcome page displays with tips on how to maximize your experience. You should record in an area with low to no echo and use your natural speaking voice.

You can pause the session at any time, save your progress, and return to it at a later time. To begin again, just click Continue.

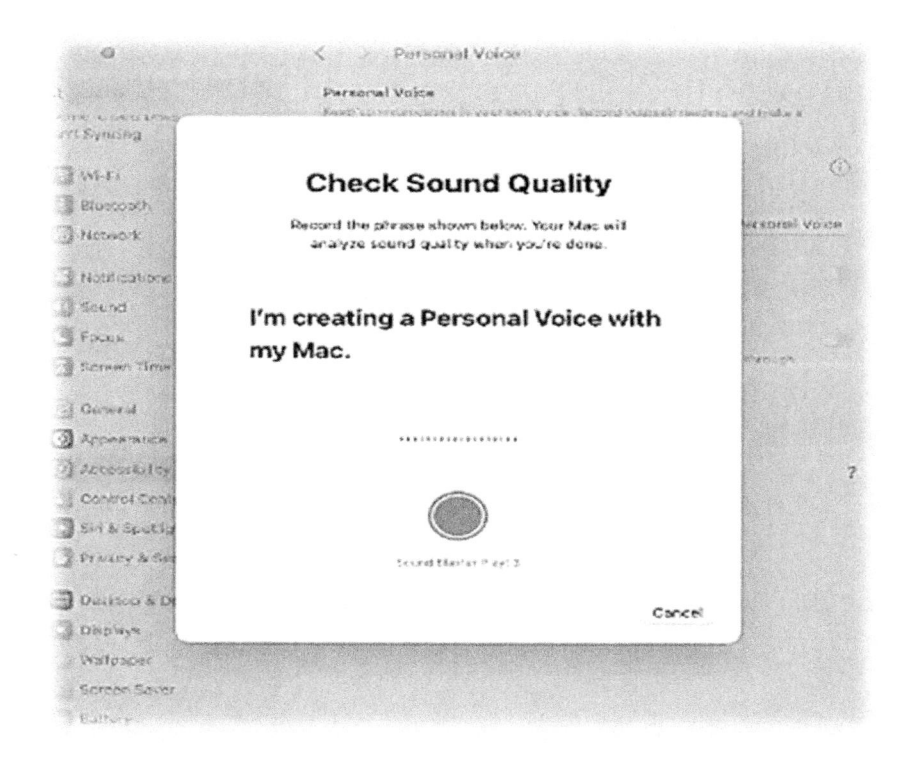

Start recording

- A voice must be given a name before recording can begin. Fill it in and hit the Next button.
- The Mac will now do a sound quality test.
- To change to another microphone, you'll have to end the current session and access the Sound System

Settings menu. If that's the case, you'll need to start from the beginning again.
- Click the red icon to continue if it corresponds to the proper microphone.
- To read the bold phrase, please click the red circle.

Keep in mind that you should use your natural conversational tone.

- The Mac will check the first recording for problems when you've finished it.
- If you notice any problems, you can fix them now and retake the test by clicking the Check Again icon.

You can choose to disregard these recommendations and proceed nonetheless.

Get this done before you start recording the first phrase.

You've reached the first display of Read the Phrase; however, you shouldn't hit the red record icon just yet. You should be aware of the following:

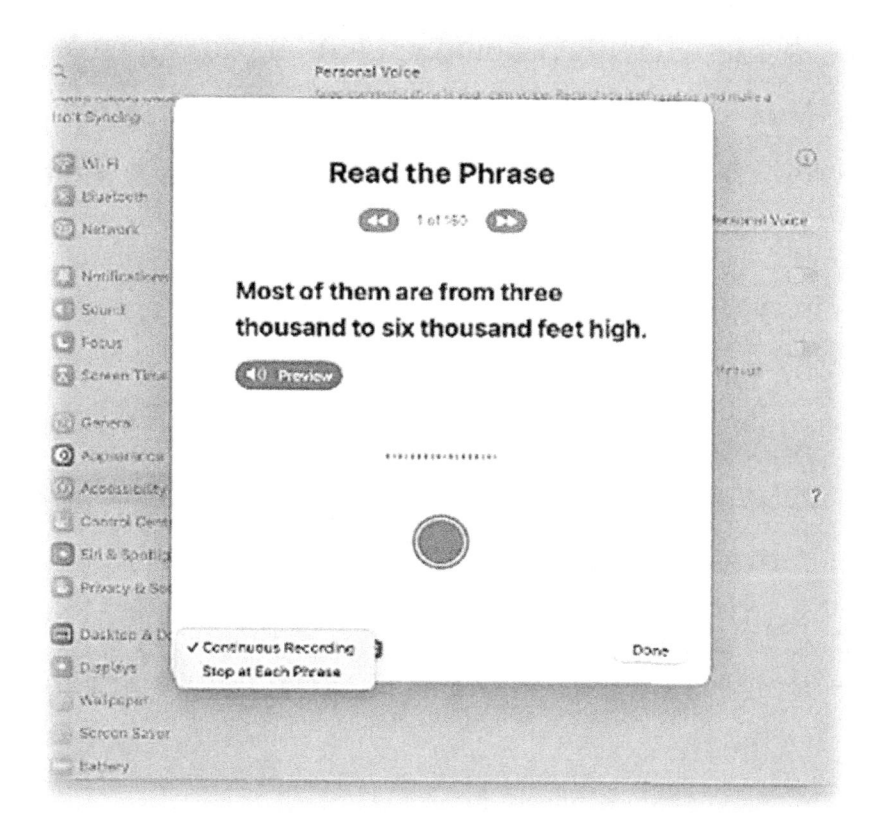

1. Your current level is shown under Read the Phrase. To return to a previous phrase, choose it and then click the left button.

To advance the list, click the appropriate icon.

2. If you want to stop reading now instead of waiting until you've read all 150 phrases, just click Done. If you leave and come back later, your spot in line will be held for you.

3. If you're having problems reading, you can have your Mac read the sentence aloud by clicking the blue Preview icon. When you're ready to repeat what you just heard, just press the red icon.

- A toggle switch in the bottom left edge toggles between two options:

1. **Continuous record:** There is no need to hit the record button between phrases since the system records continuously as you speak.
2. **End at each phrase:** Each sentence has a pause icon so you can record your voice before moving on to the next one.

Now that you know how the user interface works, you can modify it to your liking.

Initiate phrase recording.

- To begin, hit the record button. It will take around 15–20 minutes to do this.

If you make a mistake when reading a sentence and wish to try again, just click the record icon. Just hit record when you're ready to keep recording.

Pause and restart personal voice recording

Possibly you need to take a break or attend to other matters at the moment. Simply selecting "Done" will end the current session. Here's what you need to do to get your session going again:

- Find the Speech option under System Settings > Accessibility, and then choose Personal Voice.

- You'll find the amount of phrases you need to record next to the name of your personal voice under the Personal Voice heading. To learn more, choose the "i" icon.
- When prompted, type in your password in the pop-up box.
- A new window pops up with a "Keep Recording" button. The link should be clicked.
- After repeating the sound quality check, the phrase recording will resume and you can go on.

The session will stop after you have spoken the 150th phrase. You may congratulate yourself in the You're Done Recording box that displays, and then press the Continue icon.

Get Ready to Use Your Own Voice

If you're using a MacBook, plug it in now since your Mac has to get to work and it will take a long while. When the Personal Voice is complete, you will be notified.

- To proceed, just click the Done icon. Your voice-making progress will be shown in the Accessibility System Setting's Personal Voice area.

You shouldn't shut off your Mac at this time, but you can use it for other tasks. The completion date will replace the progress indicator after the procedure is complete.

Create a focus

- Launch System Preferences from the Dock or the press Apple icon and choose the System settings.
- On the left sidebar, click "Focus".

A helpful hint for maximizing work and minimizing interruptions when using a Mac's Focus modes is to turn off screenshot thumbnail previews.

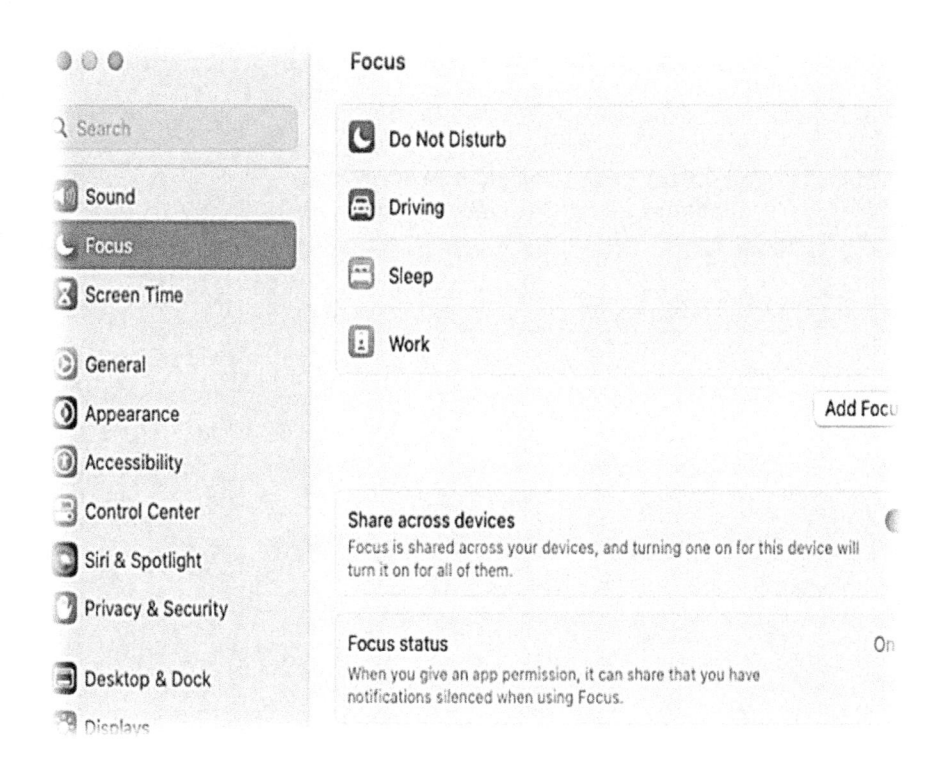

How to use focus

- To access other customization choices, choose "Add Focus" from the bottom list.
- You can choose from "Reading," "Personal," "Mindfulness," and "Games." Choose one of these, and then follow the tutorial's following steps to set it up.

Customize Focus

- Press add focus and click Custom.
- Give your Focus a name, then choose an icon color, and last, a Focus icon.

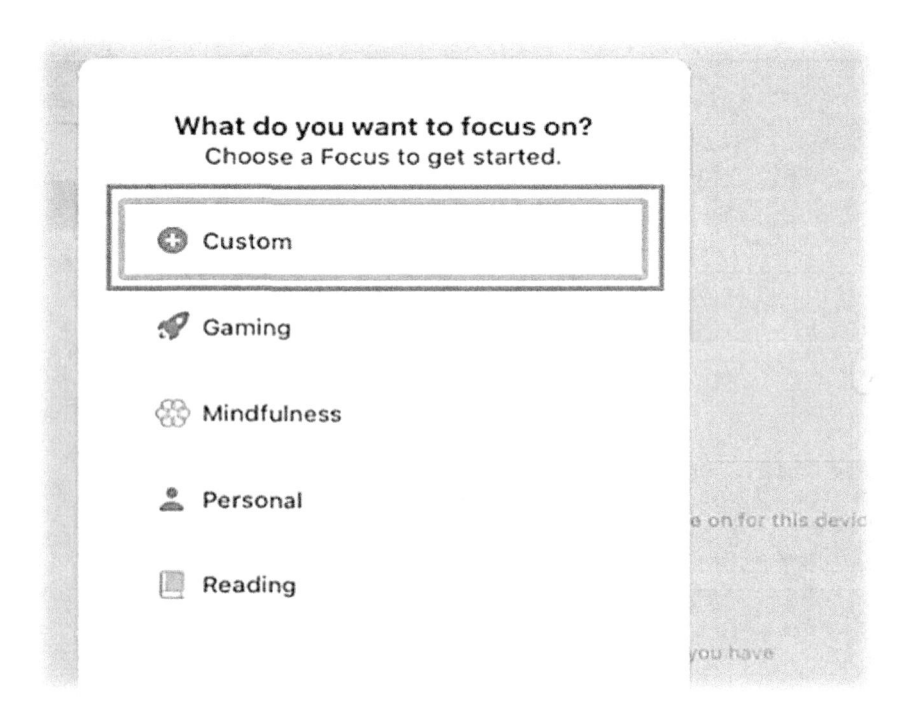

What do you want to focus on?
Choose a Focus to get started.

- Custom
- Gaming
- Mindfulness
- Personal
- Reading

- By clicking the "OK" icon, the Focus mode will be added to the collection.
- Follow the on-screen prompts to configure your new Focus.

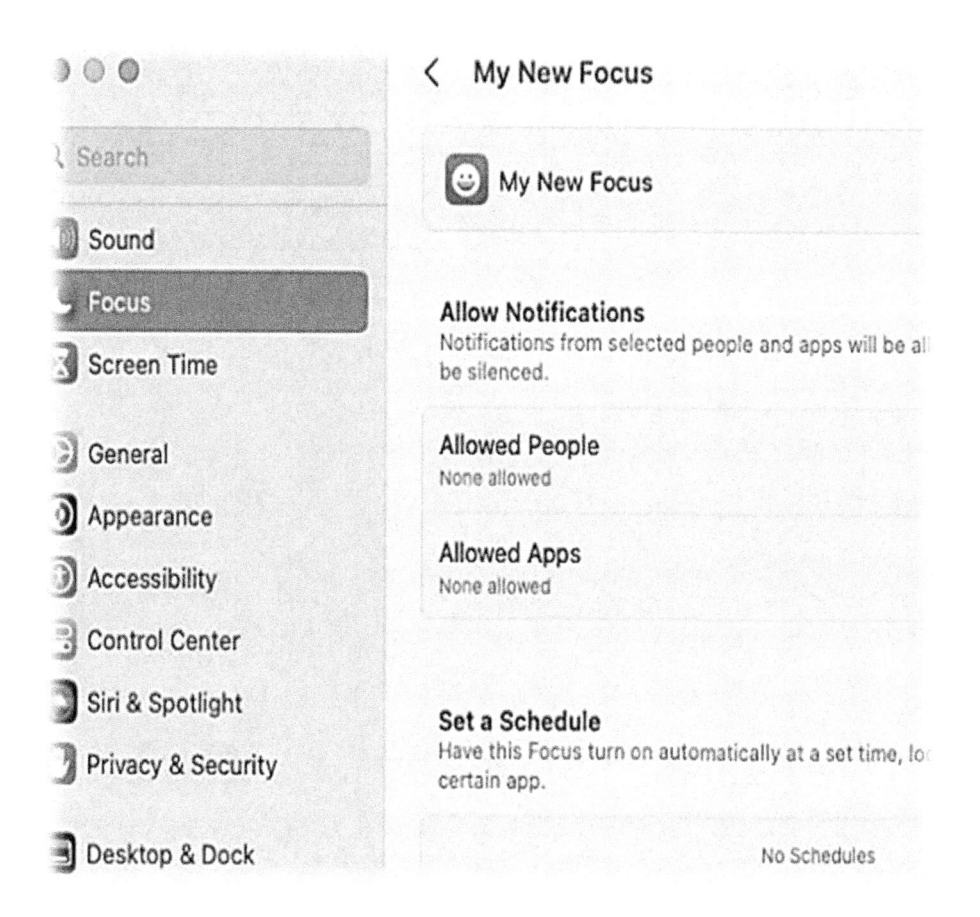

Use Focus to Enable Contact Notifications

- During your Focus time, only notifications from the people you choose under "Allowed People" will be sent to your device.

- Use the menu on the right to choose "Allow Some People" or "Silence Some People."

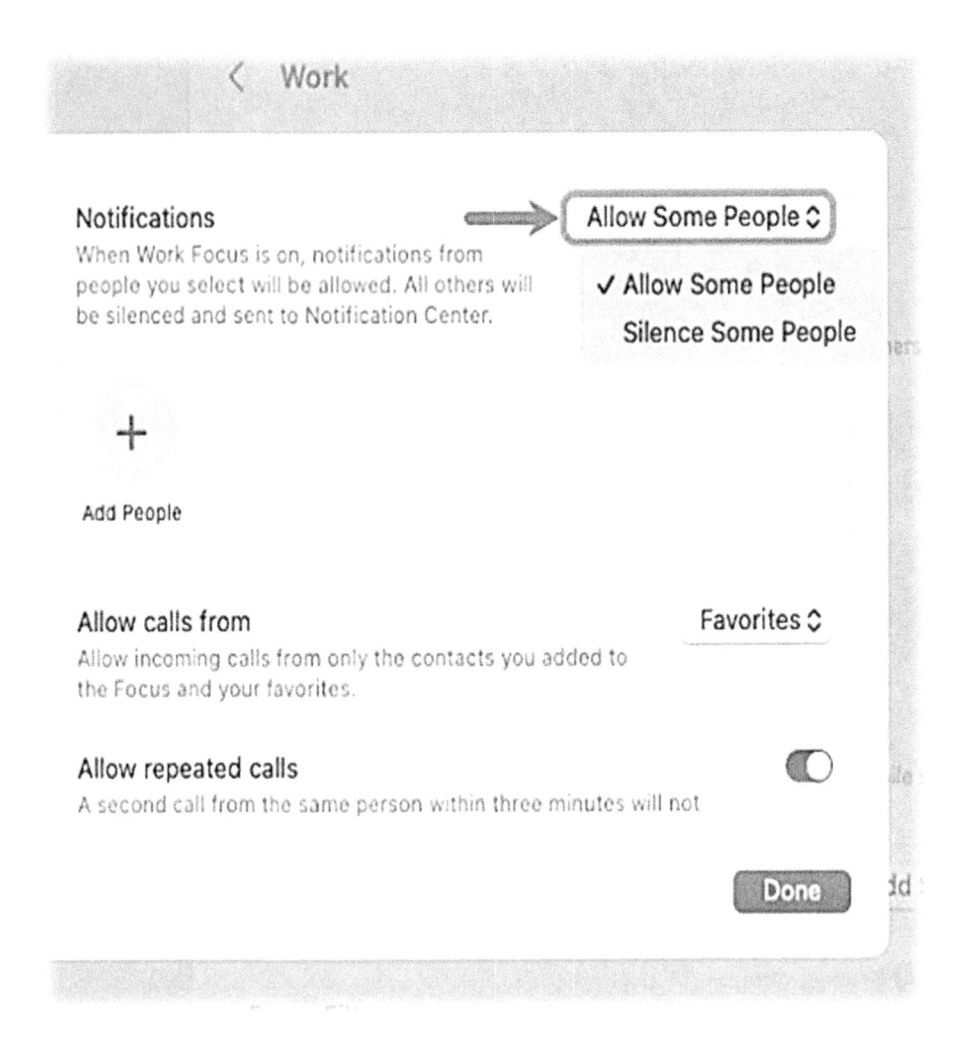

- You can add the contacts you wish to allow or mute by clicking the "Add People" icon.
- Pick a friend or colleague and hit "Add." Repeat this step for each subsequent contact you want to make.

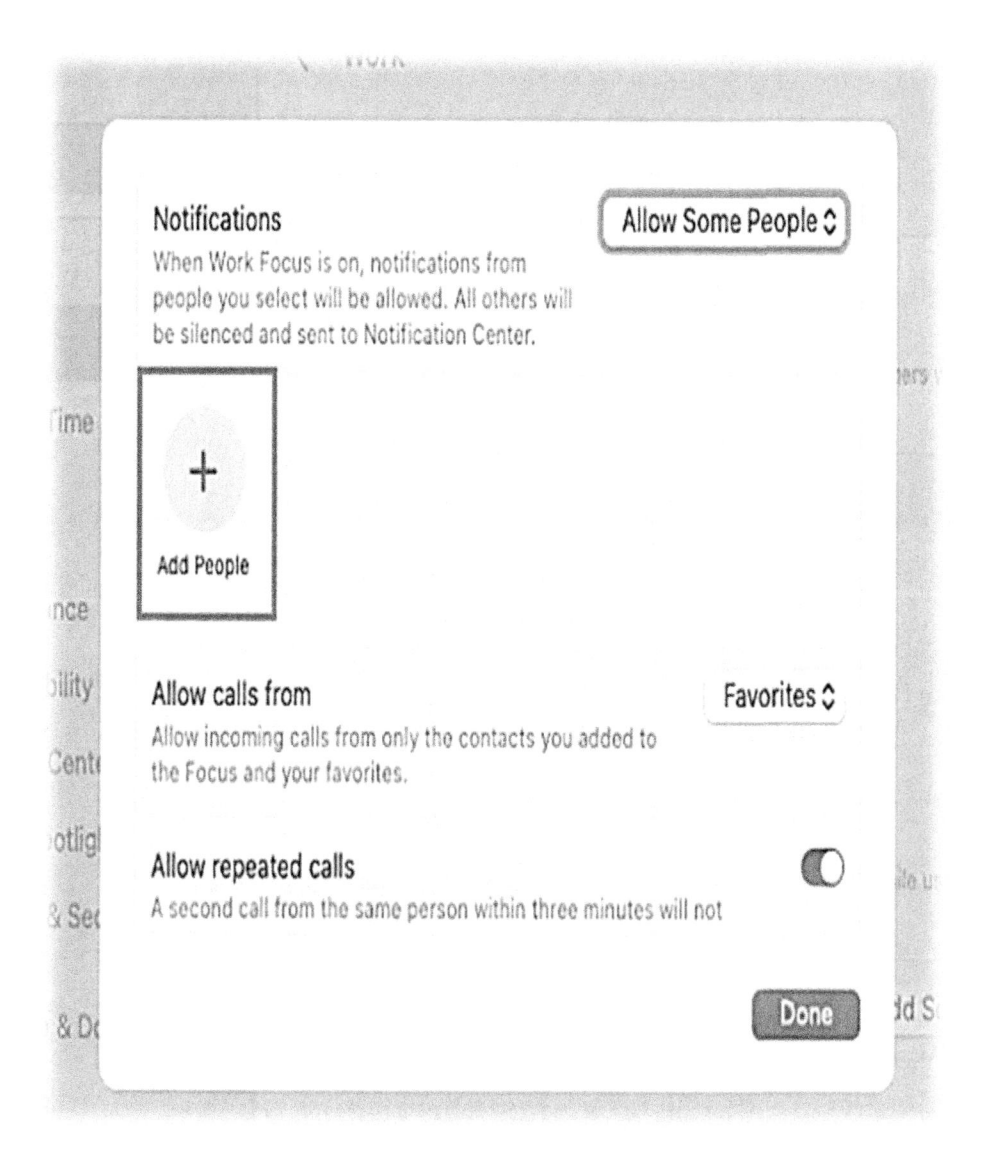

> **Notifications**
> When Work Focus is on, notifications from people you select will be allowed. All others will be silenced and sent to Notification Center.
>
> Allow Some People ⌄
>
> [+ Add People]
>
> **Allow calls from**
> Allow incoming calls from only the contacts you added to the Focus and your favorites.
>
> Favorites ⌄
>
> **Allow repeated calls**
> A second call from the same person within three minutes will not
>
> [Done]

- Select the callers you'll be accepting in the "Allow Calls From" section before beginning your Focus.
- Toggle the Calls From option to permit Focus on Mac calls.

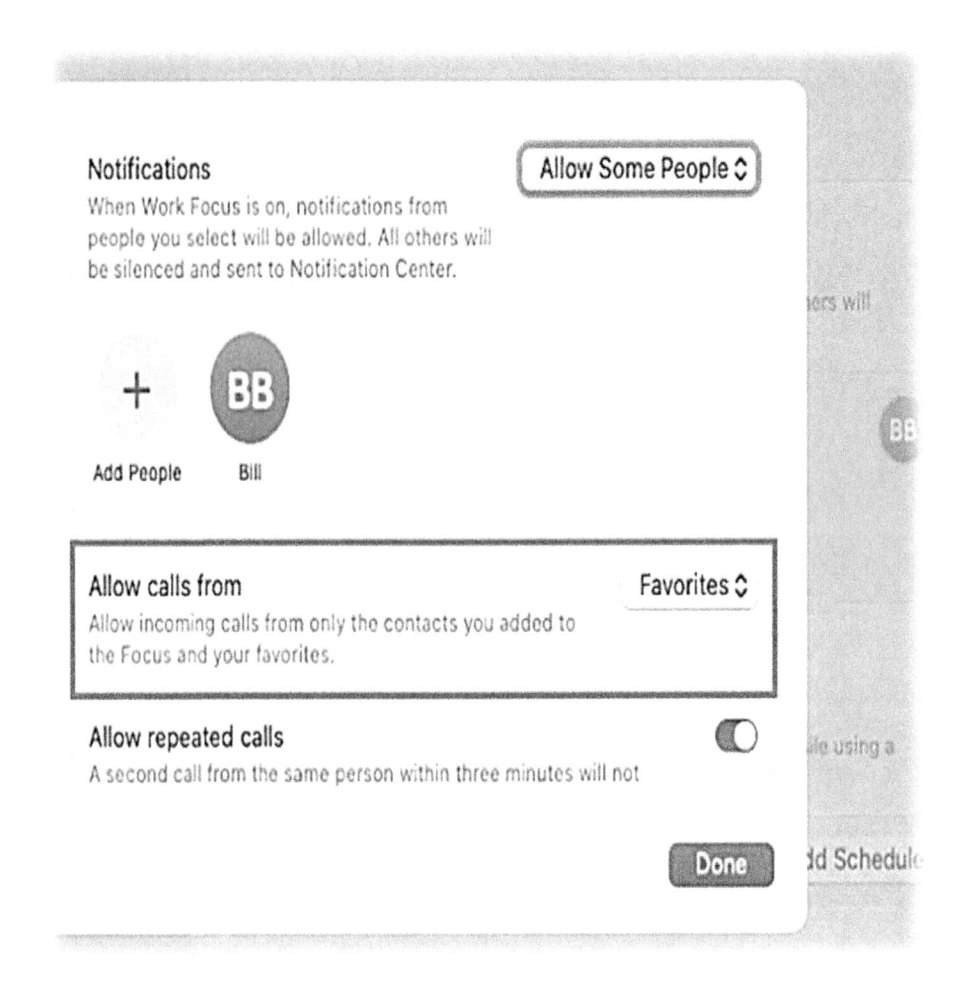

Toggle the "Allow Repeated Calls" switch on or off, as appropriate. If you switch on this feature and get another call from the same number within 3 minutes, you won't have to worry about missing either call.

- When you're through making changes, choose "Done" to apply them.

Set Apps Focus

- Choose which applications to allow notifications from and which to muzzle during your Focus time by clicking the "Allowed Apps" icon.
- Select "Allow Some Apps" or "Silence Some Apps" from the corresponding drop-down menu in the upper right.

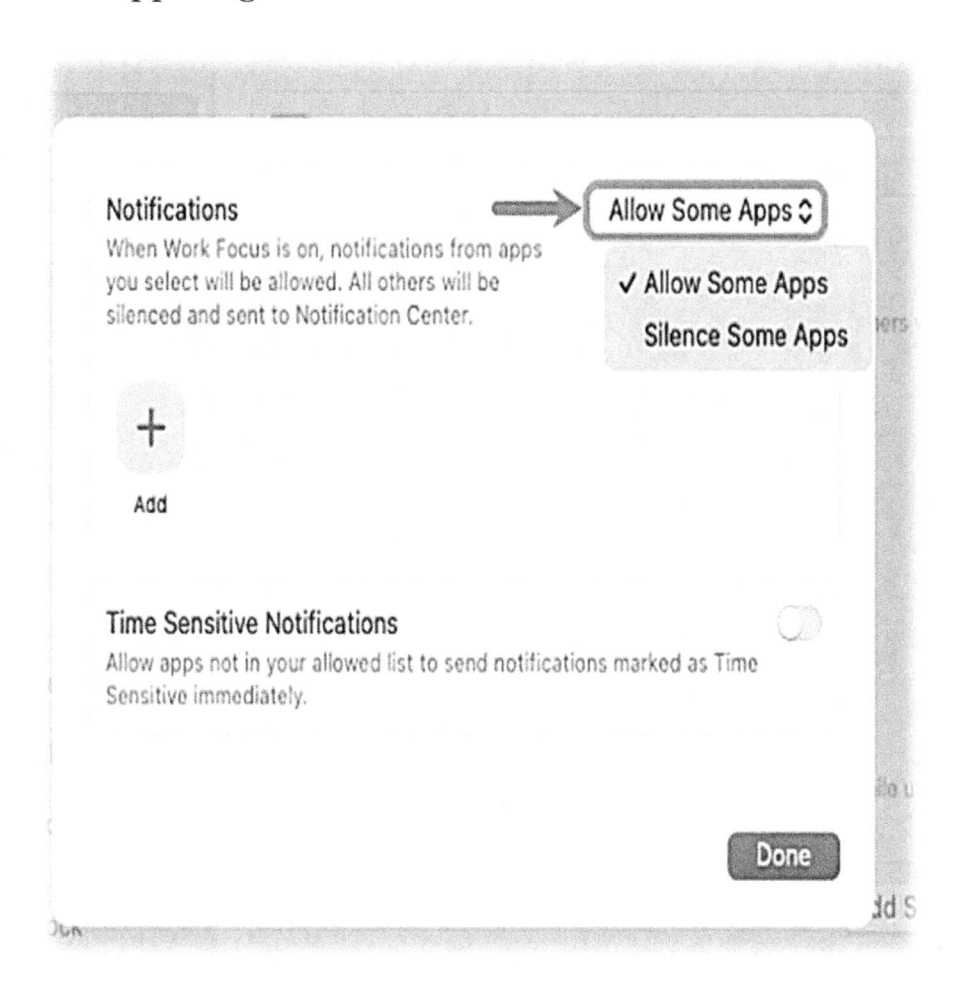

- You can add the programs you wish to hear from or ignore by clicking the "Add" button.
- Pick an app and then click "Add." Do same for other apps.

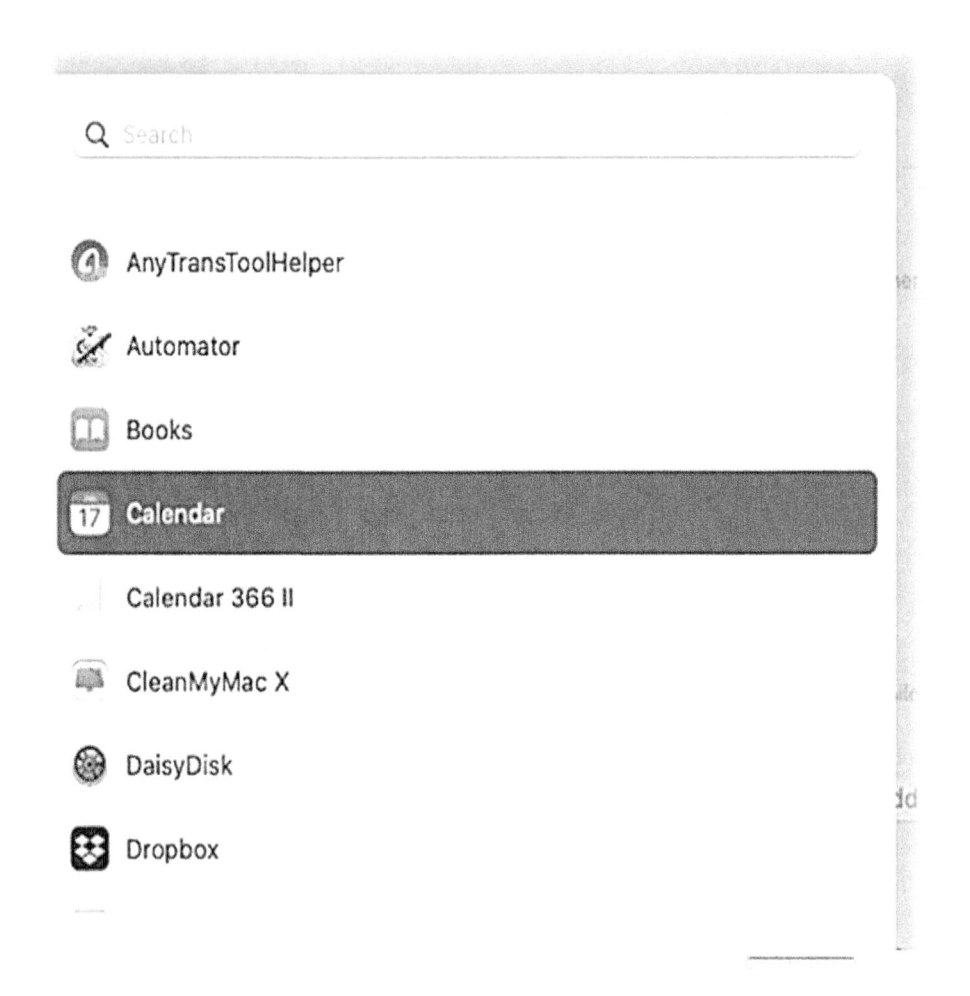

```
Q Search

   AnyTransToolHelper
   Automator
   Books
   Calendar
   Calendar 366 II
   CleanMyMac X
   DaisyDisk
   Dropbox
```

- Toggle "Time-sensitive notifications" on or off, as appropriate. Time-sensitive alerts can be sent from applications that aren't on your "Allowed" list if you toggle this option on.

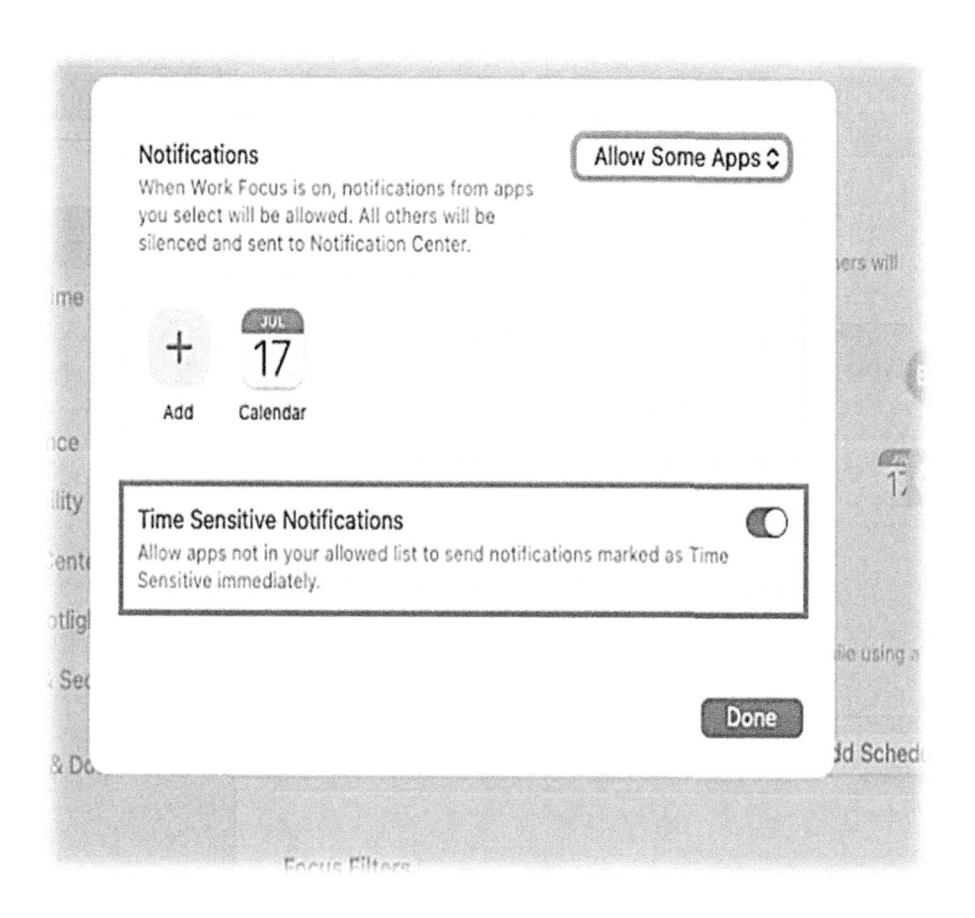

- When you're through making changes, choose "Done" to apply them.

Schedule Focus

- Look under the header "Set a Schedule," and click the "Add Schedule" icon.

100

- You can set the schedule based on time, location, or a mobile app.

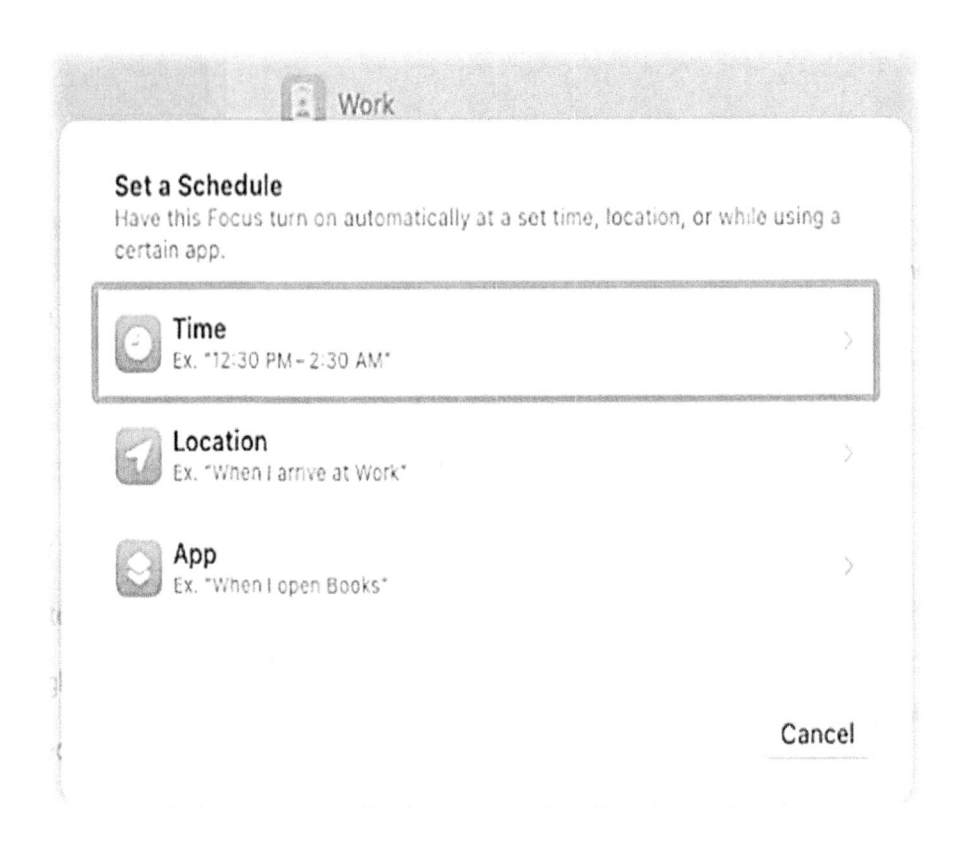

> **Work**
>
> **Set a Schedule**
> Have this Focus turn on automatically at a set time, location, or while using a certain app.
>
> **Time**
> Ex. "12:30 PM - 2:30 AM"
>
> **Location**
> Ex. "When I arrive at Work"
>
> **App**
> Ex. "When I open Books"
>
> Cancel

1. **Time:** Provide a "From" and "To" time and a repeating schedule of days of the week.
2. **Location:** The Focus can be activated by searching for a certain area and then choosing it.
3. **App:** Pick an app that automatically activates Focus.
- When you're done, go over to the "Set a Schedule" page to see your schedule.

- In the "Set a Schedule" area, choose the schedule you prefer to modify or delete, and then make any necessary modifications or click "Delete Schedule."

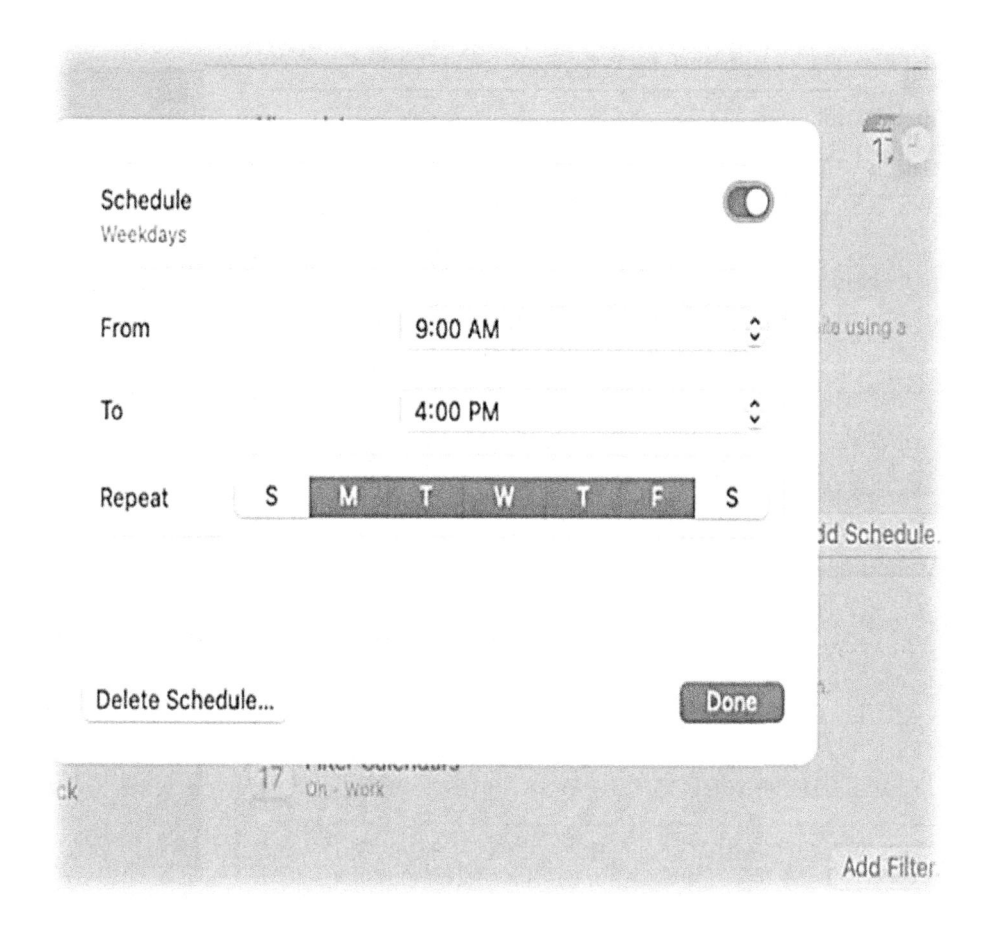

Advice: study how to make advantage of Mac's Live Text feature while working with images and video.

Set Focus Filter

- Under "Focus Filters", press Add Filter.

- When in Focus mode, you can customize the following applications' actions: Calendar, Mail, Messages, and Safari.

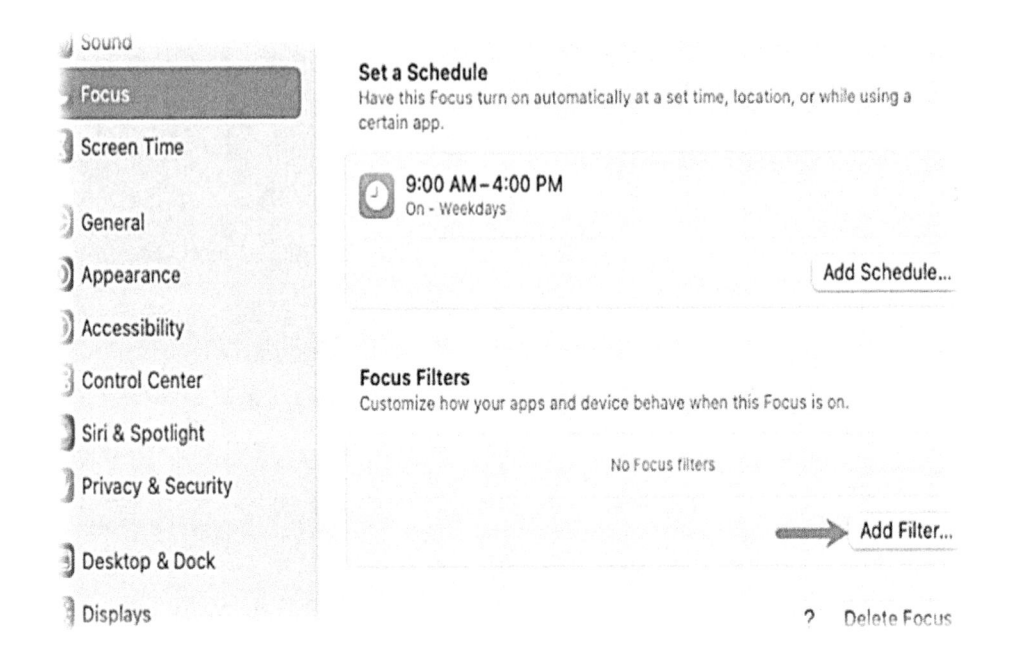

1. Focus mode calendar customization allows you to choose which calendar is shown.
2. Select which email accounts will be shown when working in Focus mode.
3. You can filter your messages to just see those from certain contacts, or you can make them visible to everyone.
4. Choose a Safari tab group that you've already created. During your Focus period in the chosen Focus Tab

Group, the toggle to access external links can also be switched on.
- Select "Add" to include the Focus Filters you've selected from the list above in your search.

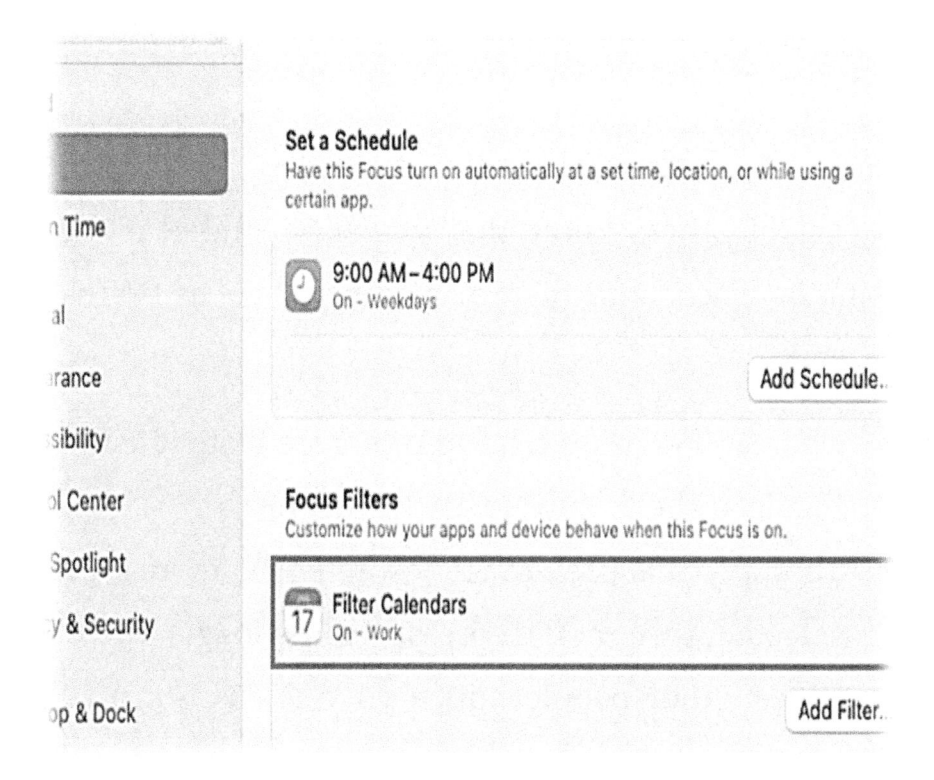

Set a Schedule
Have this Focus turn on automatically at a set time, location, or while using a certain app.

9:00 AM – 4:00 PM
On - Weekdays

Add Schedule..

Focus Filters
Customize how your apps and device behave when this Focus is on.

Filter Calendars
On - Work

Add Filter..

- Your preferences will be reflected in the Focus's "Focus Filters" section.
- Select the filter you want to update or delete from the "Focus Filters" column, then make your adjustments or click "Delete App Filter."

How to Synchronize Focus across gadgets

With the "Share across devices" switch turned on, the Focus can be accessed from any of your iOS devices in addition to your Mac. A single activation of a Focus will have an immediate effect across all of the connected devices.

Configure Focus Status

You can let others know that you have muted alerts by turning on Focus and then displaying a "Focus Status" in Messages.

- Choose "Focus Status," and then activate it using the toggle at the feature's very top.
- To apply this preference to the Focus modes you've selected, turn on the corresponding toggle.
- When other people notice your Focus Status, they have the option to still inform you.

The Focus mode you're utilizing will remain hidden from your contacts at all times.

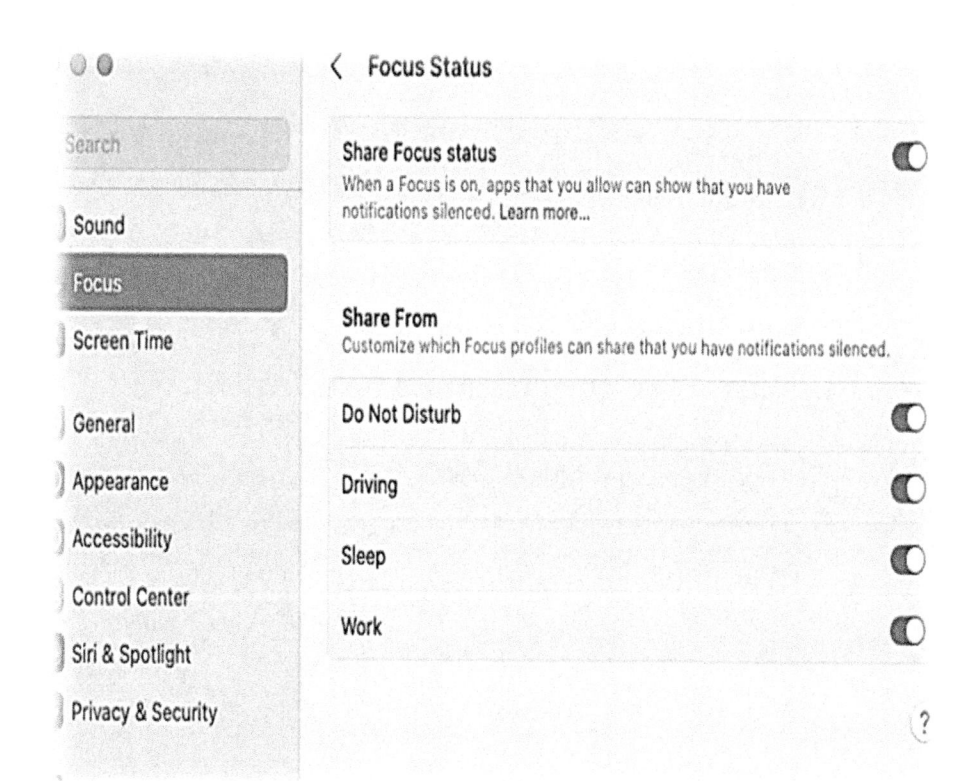

Search	**‹ Focus Status**	
Sound	**Share Focus status**	⬤
	When a Focus is on, apps that you allow can show that you have notifications silenced. Learn more...	
Focus		
Screen Time	**Share From**	
	Customize which Focus profiles can share that you have notifications silenced.	
General	Do Not Disturb	⬤
Appearance	Driving	⬤
Accessibility	Sleep	⬤
Control Center	Work	⬤
Siri & Spotlight		
Privacy & Security		?

CHAPTER 8

Activate Live Text

- Launch System settings.
- Press General.
- Press "Language & Region."
- The "Live Text" toggle should be activated.

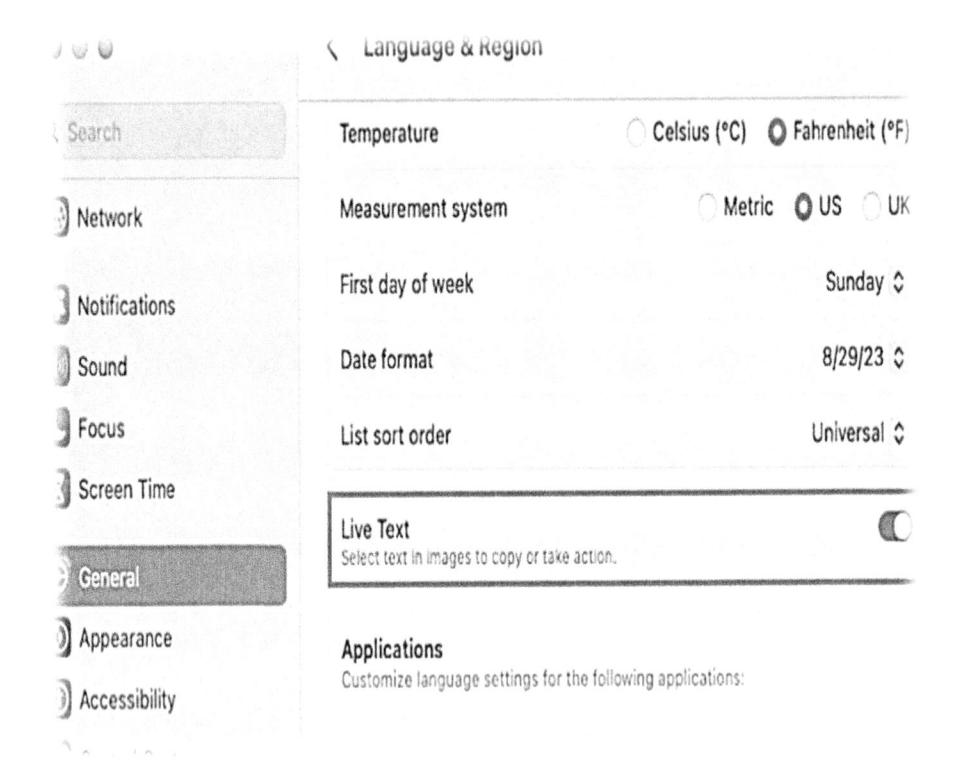

Use Live Text

- Launch Photos, double-click the image to expand it, and then press the Live text icon in the lowest right aspect.

- In the picture, the highlighted sections of text are easily visible. You can choose a fast action, such as going to a website or sending an email, or you can click "More" to view further alternatives, such as a list of addresses and phone numbers.

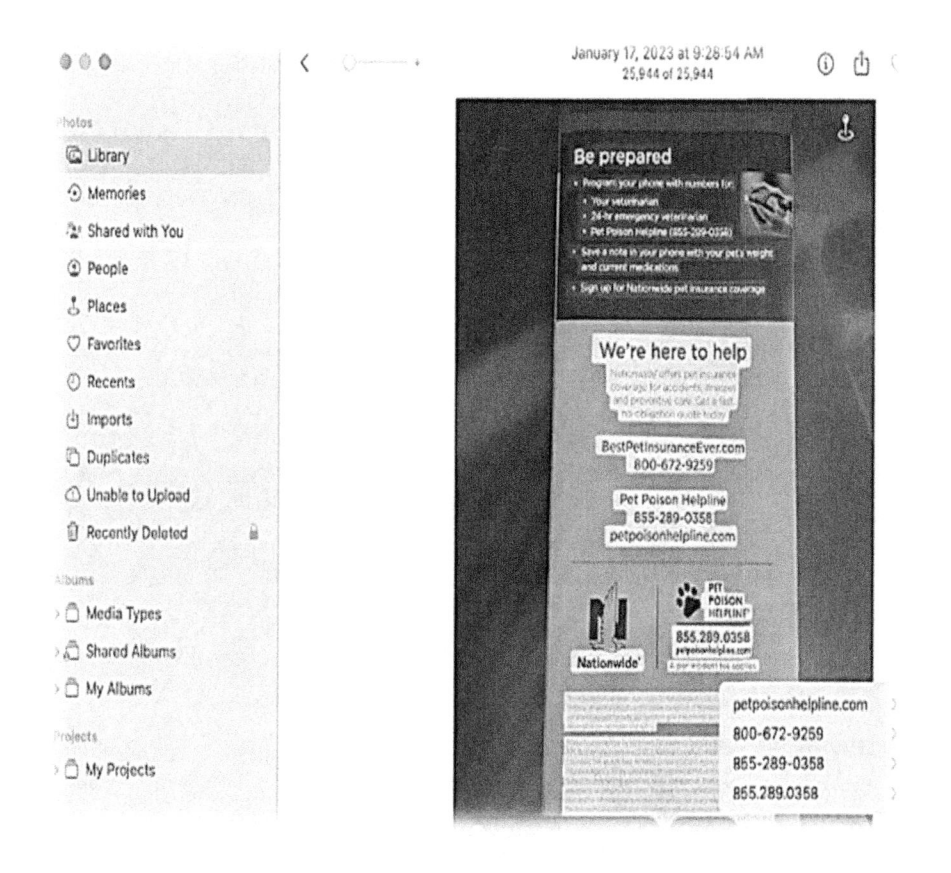

- Select text in a picture by shifting the cursor over it until it is highlighted, and then using the context menu accessible by right-clicking (or Control-clicking on a Mac) to access further editing tools.

- The highlighted text can be looked up, translated, searched, copied, or shared.

Live Text Preview App

Preview's Live Text function comes in handy when you need to add text to a screenshot or other picture.

- Launch Preview and choose the text.
- You can access look up, translating, searching, copying, and sharing the chosen text as you would in the Photos app by right-clicking or holding Control and clicking to view.

- When you place your mouse pointer over specific kinds of text—including URLs, email addresses, phone numbers, and tracking numbers—a little arrow will appear.
- When you click the arrow, you'll see options like "Add to Contacts," "Call," "Email," and "Text," among others.

Video Live Text

- Start the video and pause it when you get to the part where you want to copy and paste the text. The Live Text icon will appear on the right-hand edge of the display.
- To have the words in that particular frame of the video highlighted, click on the live text symbol. To copy everything, use the "Copy All" icon or the other shortcuts.
- You can also use the following ways to choose specific text:

1. Phone or iPad can be used to highlight text by dragging your finger over the display to one of the grab spots, tapping and holding, or using a drop-down arrow.

2. Use the grab points on a Mac to choose the text, then choose the arrow or right-click or press the control key and click.

- Select an option to do a Web-based copy, translation, lookup, sharing, or web search on the selected text.

Use Mac to Make and receive calls

On macOS: Select FaceTime, press Preferences > Settings > calls.

Open the iOS Settings menu, tap Phone, and then tap Allow Calls from Other Devices. Toggle the switch for the targeted Mac in the same place.

- You will now be alerted on your Mac whenever you get a call on your phone. You'll be able to answer or ignore the call directly from the alert.
- Simply Control-clicking a phone number or link to a phone number in any Mac software will initiate a call. The next step is to choose the Call option.
- The message "Call this number using your iPhone: [Number]" will then display. To make a call, just click the number.

Using Your Mac to Send and Receive Text

- If you activate Text Message Forwarding in Settings > Messages on your iPhone, you'll be able to send texts from your Mac.

You must also check your iMessage phone number and inbox often to make sure you can be reached. To accomplish this, under the Messages app's settings, indicate the appropriate contact information:

- Click Messages > Preferences > Accounts in the menu bar on your Mac.
- In the iOS Settings, Select Messages then click Send & Receive.

You can now use your Mac to send and receive SMS messages. You can test this out by launching an iMessage chat as usual and seeing whether you have the option to enter a phone number as the recipient this time around. You should be able to do this with the help of text forwarding.

Set Up FaceTime On Mac

- Open System settings and then choose Sign In at the upper part of the sidebar if you have an Apple ID.

- Click Create Apple ID on the Sign In screen if you haven't already set up an Apple ID.

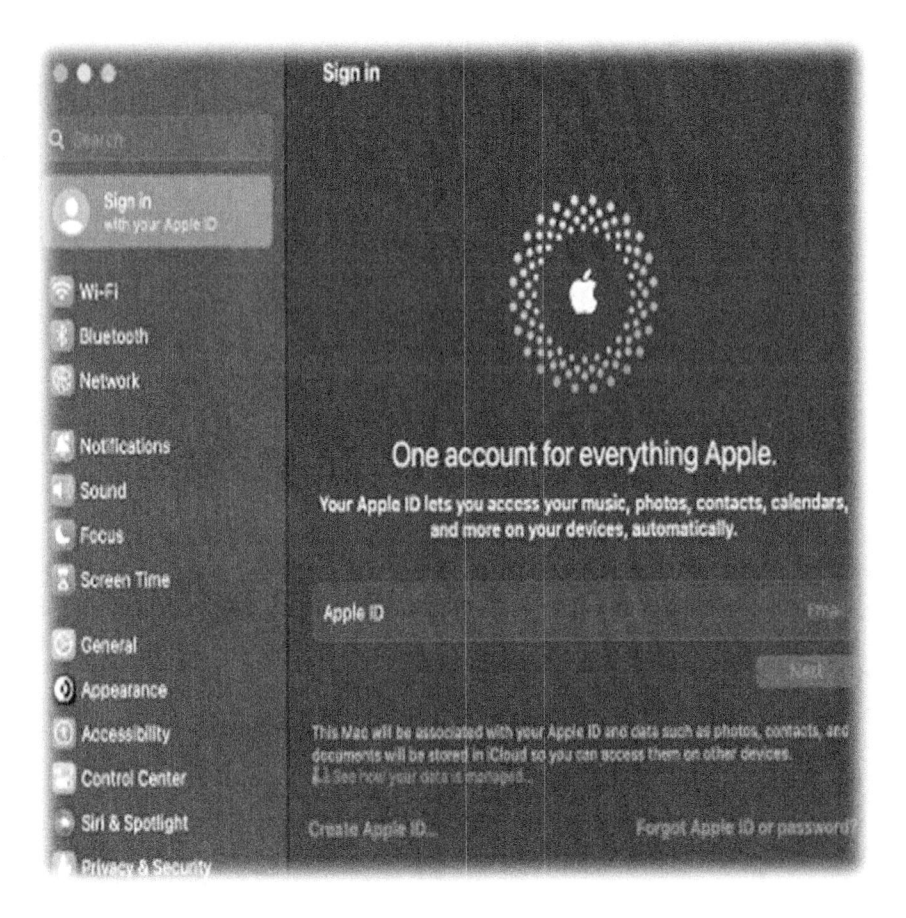

- You could also use FaceTime directly from the Dock or Launchpad, where you could sign in with an existing Apple ID or create a new one.

- After logging in with your Apple ID, FaceTime calls can be made and received on your Mac.

Make FaceTime call

- Click the video camera icon in the Dock (or Launchpad) to open FaceTime.
- Choose New FaceTime and then enter the contact's name, mobile number, or email address.

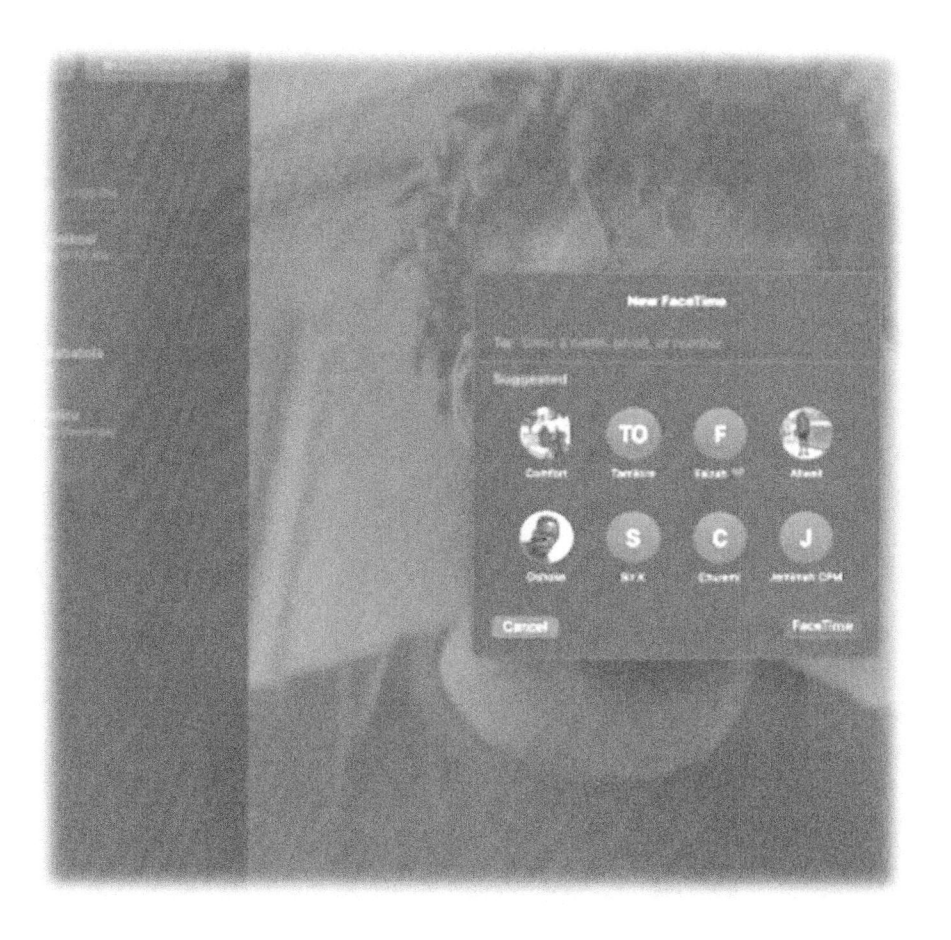

- The call should join as soon as you click FaceTime.

A few things should be kept in mind while using the FaceTime app:

1. Multiple people can join a FaceTime call at once.
2. Contact information that has not been associated with an Apple ID will be displayed in green. If you continue, FaceTime will send them an SMS with a link to your video call. This technique can be used to do Mac FaceTime with people who are not using an Apple.

- If you want to make a FaceTime Audio call instead of a video call, just click the arrow next to the FaceTime icon.
- Also, make FaceTime call using your iPhone (if you have another nearby device logged into the same Apple ID) from the options menu.

Asking Siri to call someone from your contact list can also initiate a FaceTime call. Say "Place a FaceTime Audio call" if you wish to use the audio component of a FaceTime call.

Create a FaceTime Link
- Press the Create Link icon.

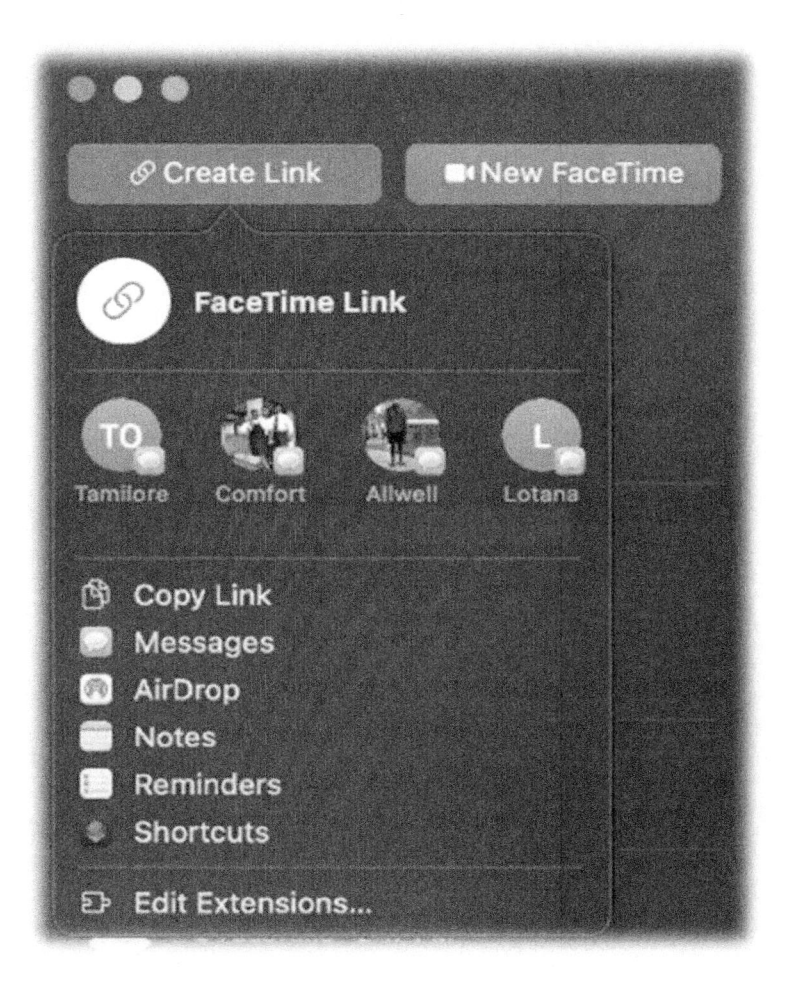

- Simply copy the URL to your clipboard by clicking the button provided.
- Select Messages from the drop-down menu to send it by text message.

FaceTime Video Effects

The "Portrait" effect in FaceTime videos focuses on your face while blurring the surroundings.

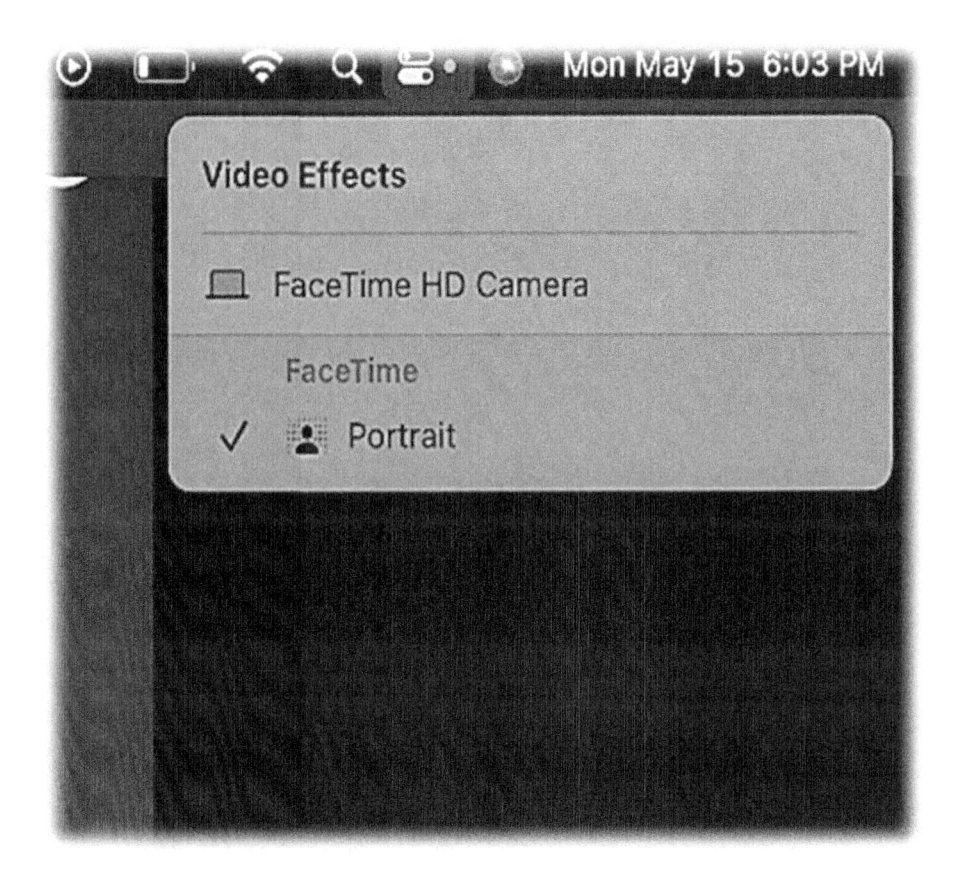

- Select Video Effects from the Control Center menu while on a video call to activate. The Mac also has a Portrait mode that can be used with any program.

FaceTime screen sharing

- Open FaceTime.
- To make a call, either pick New FaceTime or a recently used contact and click Call.
- Select the SharePlay button after the call is connected.

- To share just a single window or your complete desktop, choose Window or Screen, respectively. Selecting Window will prompt you to pick an application from which to share.
- Your FaceTime call participants will be able to see the window or display you shared until you close it.

Change FaceTime Camera and Microphone
- Get your gadget connected to your Mac.
- Launch FaceTime.
- Choose Video from the main menu to see your available hardware.

- Choose the camera, microphone, and output device you want to use from the menu's drop-down options.
- Use external gadgets to boost the quality of your FaceTime sessions, both visual and audio.

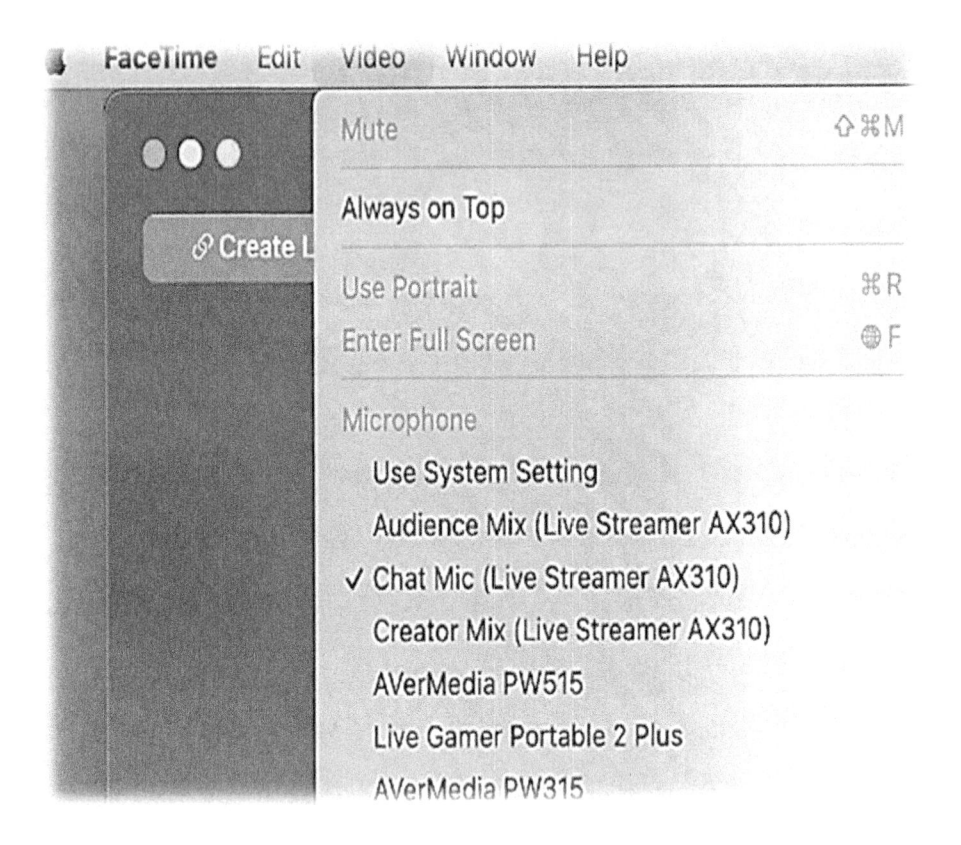

Set Screen Timeout

To modify the amount of time your Mac's display remains on, click the Apple menu icon in the top menu bar.

- Press the Apple logo on Mac.
- Go to system Settings.

- Press Battery.
- Set the timer for when you don't want the display to go dark by dragging the slider under "Turn display off after."
- If you want the same rule to apply when your Mac is plugged in as when it isn't, click Power Adapter and repeat the previous steps.

CHAPTER 9

Disable Screen Timeout

- Select the Apple icon.
- Press System Preference.
- Click Battery.

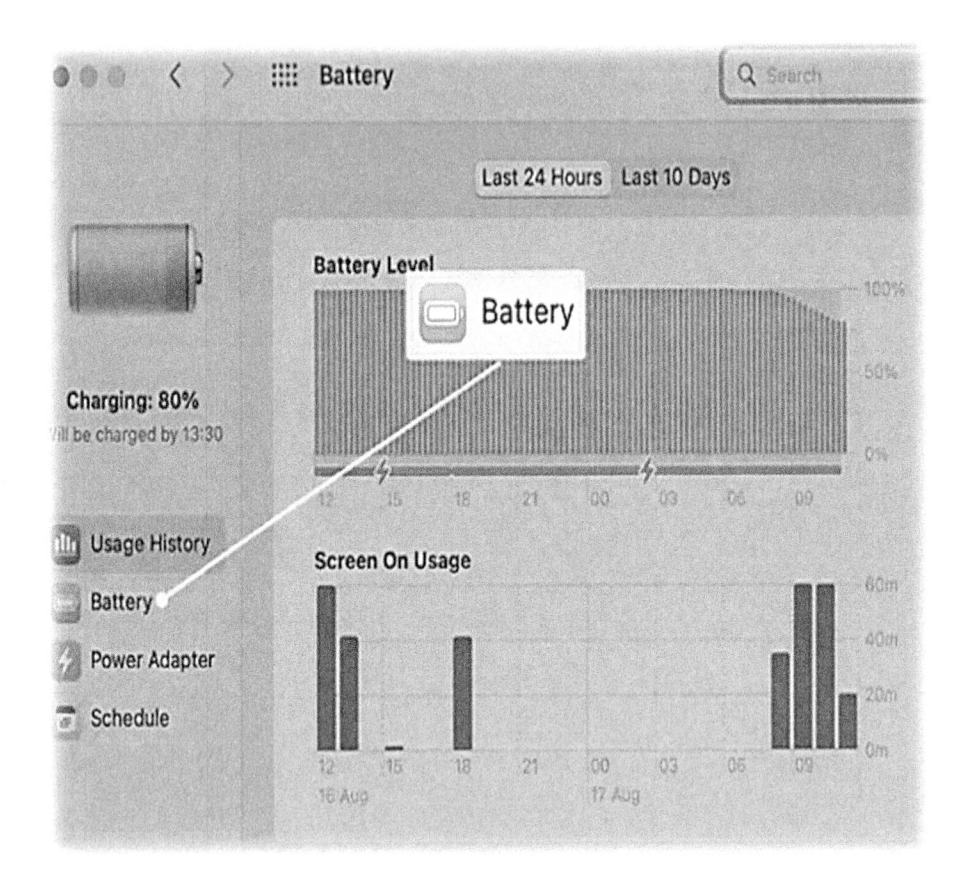

- Battery is emphasized in the Mac's System Preferences.
- The slider should be set to Never.

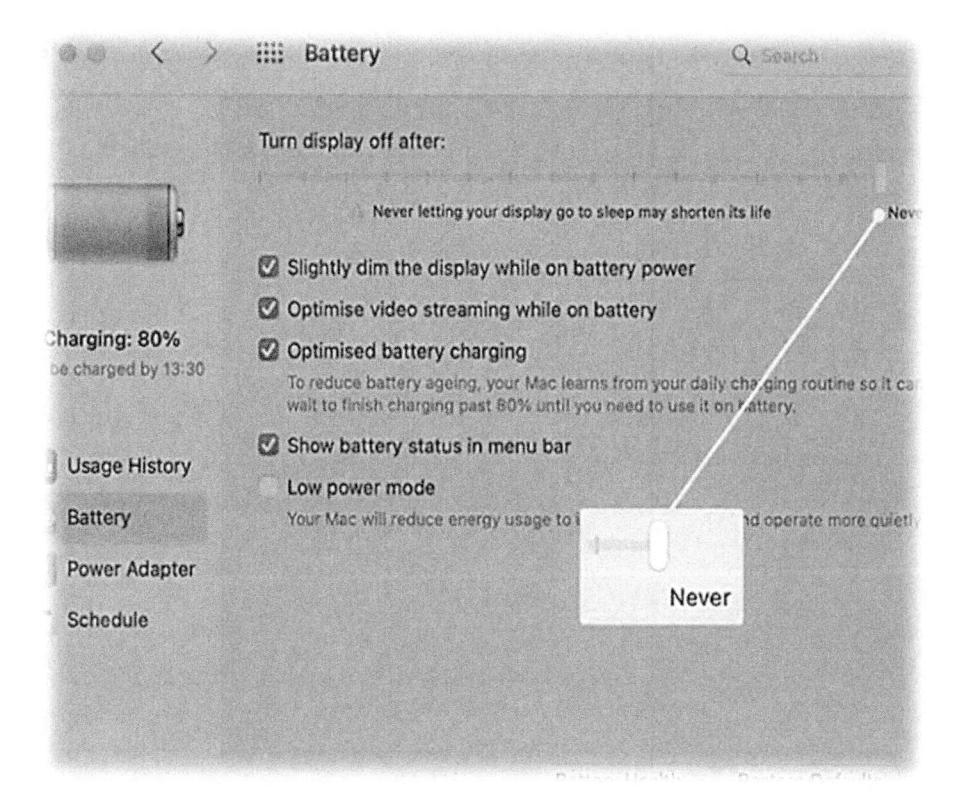

- Select the power adapter and do it again.

Explore screen-sharing app

- Open Screen Sharing app.
- Select from previously shared connections.
- Press the + symbol in the upper right.
- Connect to a display by entering the owner's Apple ID.
- Wait fora acceptance.

Screen Sharing

is requesting permission to share your screen.

If you are not sure who william.gallagher@icloud.com is, do not allow them to share your screen.

Allow user to: ○ Control my screen
User can take full control of your computer.

○ Observe my screen
User can view your screen but not control it.

Block This User   Decline   Accept

- When this occurs, you will be able to take control of their Mac from your own.

Almost everything about that procedure is the same as it was in macOS Ventura; however, there is one key distinction. There used to be nothing more than a dialogue window that prompted you to enter the other person's Apple ID whenever you ran Screen Sharing. A history of your connections is now shown. You can use its editing features to remove contacts or organize them into other categories. However, the experience for the other user remains unchanged. What they see is:

- An indication for connection.
- The notice includes buttons to click to either accept or decline the connection.
- Then, a window with further customization choices

The Accept and Decline buttons are options, but you now have the ability to set a time restriction on the connection or completely deny access to the connected user.

Sharing your display with another person gives them the option to either Control my screen or Observe my screen. The latter just allows them to watch your hands while you show them how to accomplish something. If you choose the former, it will be as if they were sitting in front of your Mac and had complete control over it.

End Screen Sharing

An additional icon appears in the user's menu bar after display sharing has begun. The option to stop sharing the screen can be found there. They also can pause the sharing.

Use Video call reactions

Camera-based automated reactions

- In macOS Sonoma, you can join a video call using Zoom, FaceTime, or almost any other service.

- Make one of the chosen gestures motion toward the camera.
- Wait.
- See the digital visuals play out in the space behind, in front of, and all around you.

Apple says you can take use of these automated responses "when using the built-in camera on Mac computers with Apple Silicon, or any Mac when using Continuity Camera with iPhone 12 and later."

However, tests showed that even with a third-party camera attached to the Mac, automated responses were identified. However, the Reactions functionality will most certainly not run on Intel Macs. When it comes to the responses themselves, in all but one instance, the digital animation overlay vanishes on its own after a few seconds. So far, only raising your hand to speak has been an exception to this rule.

After doing so, the Mac will activate Zoom's digital on-display hand-raised image. There doesn't appear to be an Undo gesture, so the raised hand will remain on display until you click the Zoom app. In principle, the necessary physical gestures are the most efficient means of communication. It's common practice to indicate agreement with a choice by indicating it with two thumbs up.

When you do the thumbs-up gesture, a succession of blue forms will appear and eventually coalesce into the thumbs-up icon. All of these features can be accessed during a Zoom call without the need for any additional software or hardware.

Selecting Reactions Manually

However, you do have a backup plan in case reaction-spotting does not improve in speed. It's a back-up plan for when you forget which gesture goes with which. It's the new app in the menubar where you can manually access the Reactions panel.

This app is always available in macOS Sonoma and serves different purposes depending on the apps you operating and the tasks you're performing. For instance, the app will provide choices when you're voice recording using a live microphone.

When you are participating in a Zoom call, the app in the menu bar will transform to provide a pop-out tray with available reactions.

There are presently eight different responses available, such as thumbs up and thumbs down, as well as iOS-style icons like balloons. Any one of the eight can be activated with a click of its symbol, and the corresponding response will show in your video chat instantly.

Configure screen saver

The screensaver selection is the same as the wallpaper selection. Screensavers with animations are clearly marked so that you can tell them apart from static wallpaper. Take these steps to install a screensaver on your computer.

- Enter settings.
- Find Wallpaper in the drop-down option and choose it.
- Locate a screensaver that has a play button.
- Pick it to be your default wallpaper and screen saver.
- You have the option of setting it as both your screensaver and backdrop or only the latter.

How to Use Center Stage

- Select the new menu button while on the video conference.
- You can either activate center stage, or
- To access further controls, if any, press the arrow to the right of the stage's center position.

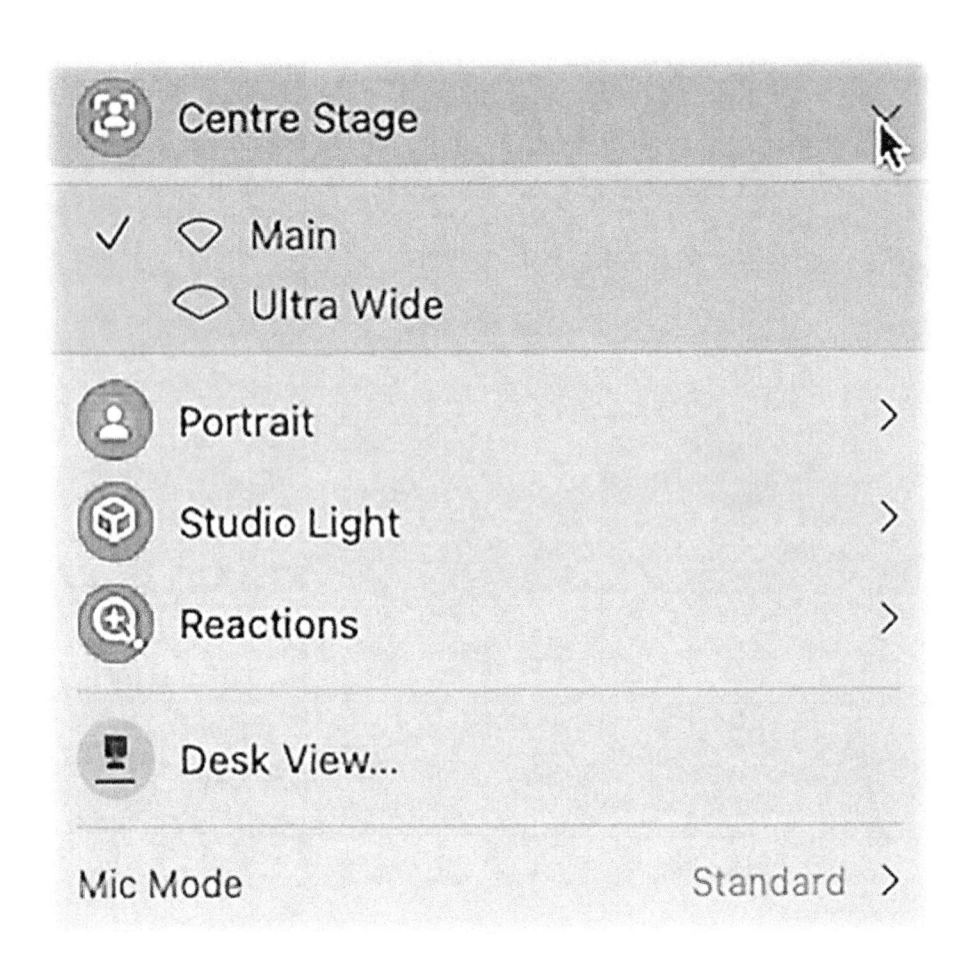

Center Stage was a checkbox in macOS Ventura's Preferences menu. Toggle the functionality by clicking the icon labeled "Center Stage."

Use Handoff

- A Handoff icon for the app you're using on your iPhone should appear in the Dock of your Mac while you're using Handoff.

- A little phone will float in the top right edge of a gray circle, much like the standard app icon.

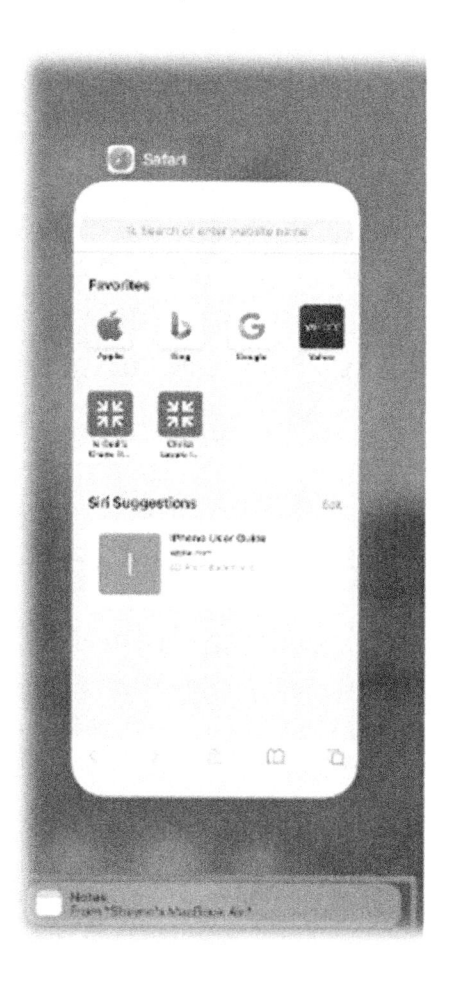

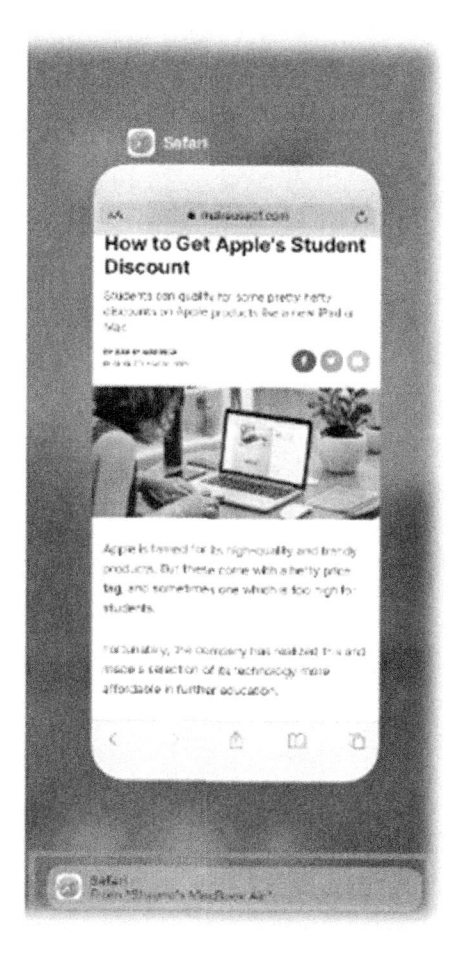

- If you're picking up where you left off on an iPhone, click that icon.

This Handoff symbol is not shown when syncing data between a Mac and an iPhone. A banner ad for your app will instead show up in the App Switcher.

Switch on AirPlay

- Select Screen Mirroring from the menu bar's Control Center icon.
- Select the TV you wish to mirror to or utilize As Separate Display, depending on how you want to utilize the receiving display.
- To deactivate AirPlay, return to the Control Center and choose display Mirroring from the menu. To disable AirPlay, choose the name shown for the receiving device.

AirPlay from Mac to iOS Devices

- To activate AirPlay, choose the icon from the Mac's menu bar.

- Select your iOS device from the drop-down menu, in this case, an iPhone or iPad.
- If a passcode prompt displays, enter it on your Mac.
- Pick the device you want to use to mirror your Mac's screen.

AirPlay on TV with Mac

- First, open System Preferences by selecting the Apple menu item if the Screen Mirroring icon is not already there.

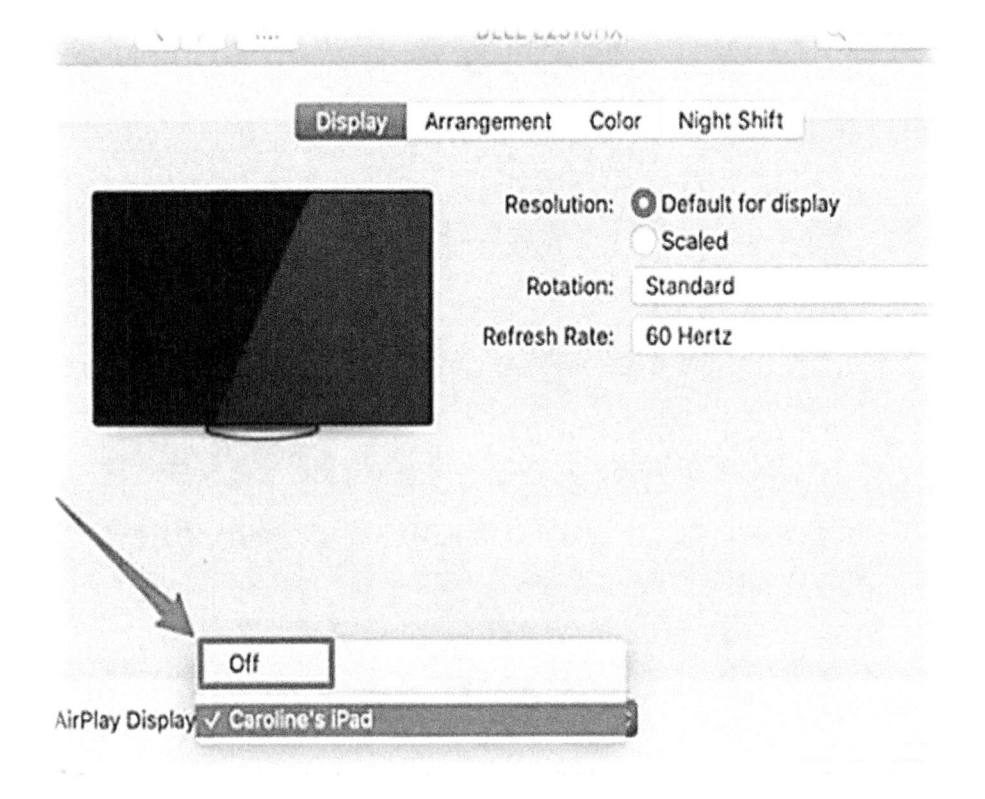

- Pick Control Center from the left menu, and then make sure the Always Show in Menu Bar checkbox is checked next to Screen Mirroring.
- Select your listed Smart TV and pick the Screen Mirroring option.
- To cast your Mac to your Smart TV, enter the 4-digit AirPlay code that displays on your TV.

To stop the AirPlay mirroring from your Mac to TV, choose the symbol that looks like a TV and then click the display name again. You can no longer send what's on your Mac to the TV display.

Listen to Podcasts

Use the following filters to narrow your search for a podcast in the Apps left-hand sidebar.

Listen Now: Check out what's in your Up Next queue, explore new channels, explore recommendations based on your listening habits, and more!

Browse: Examine podcasts by category, season, or other filter, such as "New & Noteworthy," "Featured Channels," "Shows We Love," and so on.

Top Charts: Check out the most popular podcasts and episodes by browsing the Top Charts section of the Podcasts app.

- Pick a program or episode to hear. The length, description, and title can all be seen.

To hear it, just click the Play or Latest Episode button. The Podcasts app has a toolbar at the upper part where you can access playback options.

1. The left side of the player controls playback and skips forward and backward.
2. The name of the program or episode appears in the middle, and a slider allows you to quickly go to a certain time.
3. To the right, you'll find controls for adjusting the volume, sharing the current track through AirPlay, learning more about the track, and seeing your Up Next queue.

- Save, download, and/or share the podcasts you like. To access the shortcuts, open the episode description page and look to the top right.

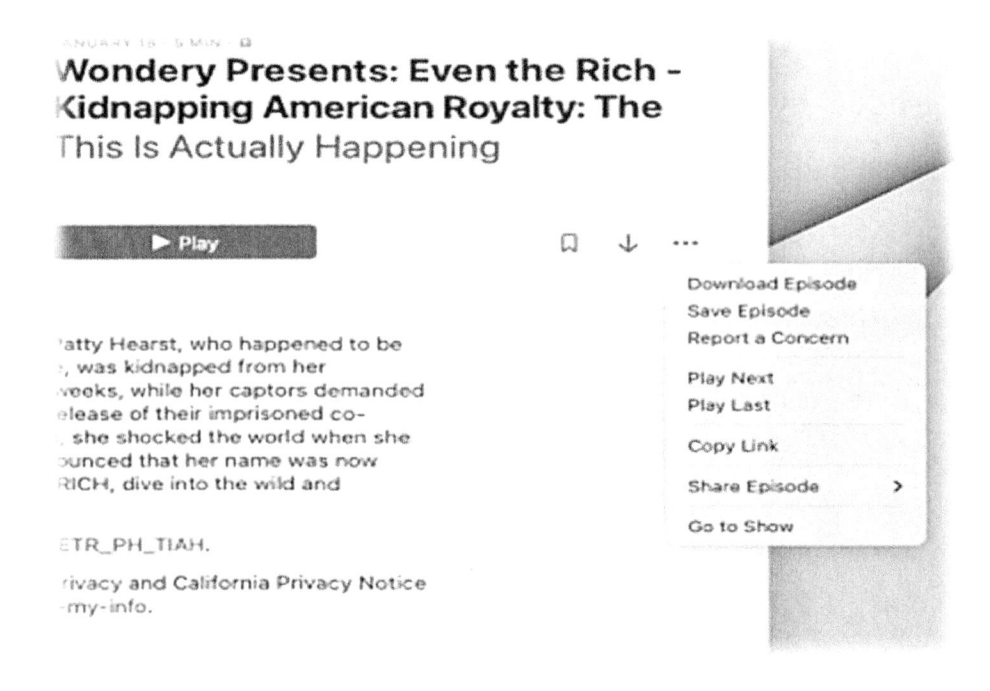

1. You can bookmark the episode by clicking the star.
2. To save the episode to your computer, click the download option.
3. To play the next track, mark this one as played, or share it with friends, just tap the three dots.

In the sidebar, you can access your Shows, Recently Played, Downloaded, and Most Recent Episodes.

- Make use of these Podcasts app's additional functions:
1. Keep up with your favorite programs by following them.
2. Make your own Stations to keep track of all your favorite programs. These are analogous to Apple Music playlists.
3. To set up automatic downloads, customize the skip button timings, and synchronize with your Apple devices, go to Podcasts > Preferences.

CHAPTER 10
Create Safari Tab Group

- To create a new tab group in Safari, open the Show Sidebar menu by clicking the symbol that looks like a set of traffic lights.
- Select New Empty Tab Group or New Tab Group with X Tabs from the menu close to the Show Sidebar symbol. Here, X is the number of the tab you presently have open.
- If you want a new Tab Group, type the name and hit Enter.

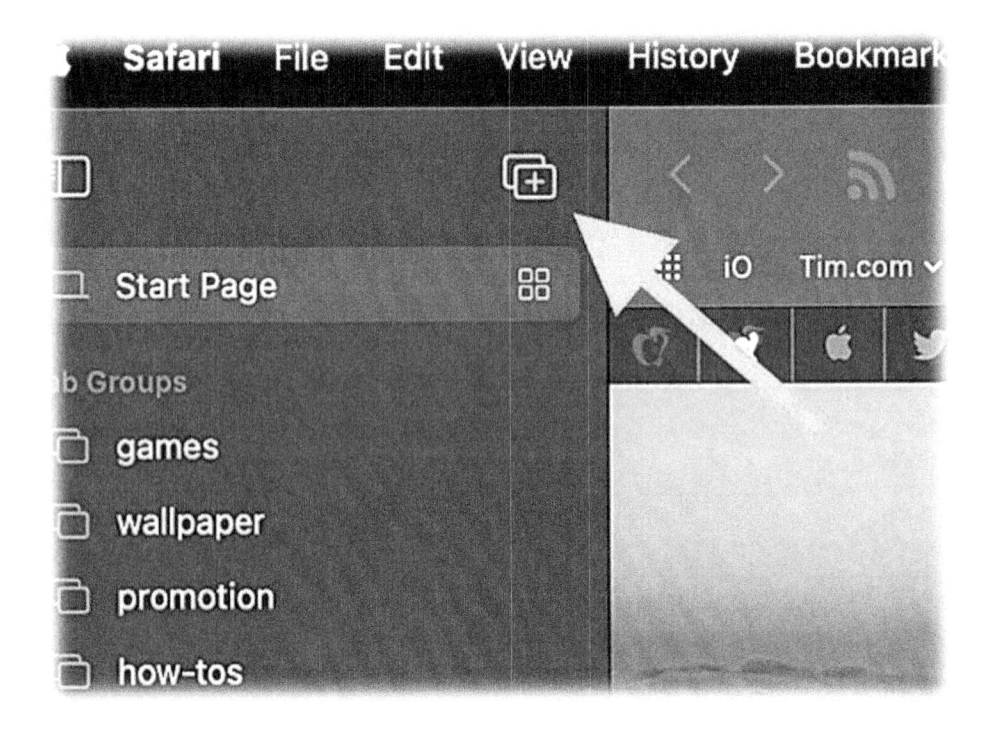

You can quickly navigate between Tab Groups using the list that appears in the sidebar. Groups can also be chosen by using the drop-down menu next to the sidebar symbol. Each new tab you open after choosing a Tab Group will be added to that group.

View All Safari tabs group

Take these steps will give you a bird's eye view of all the tabs in a given set.

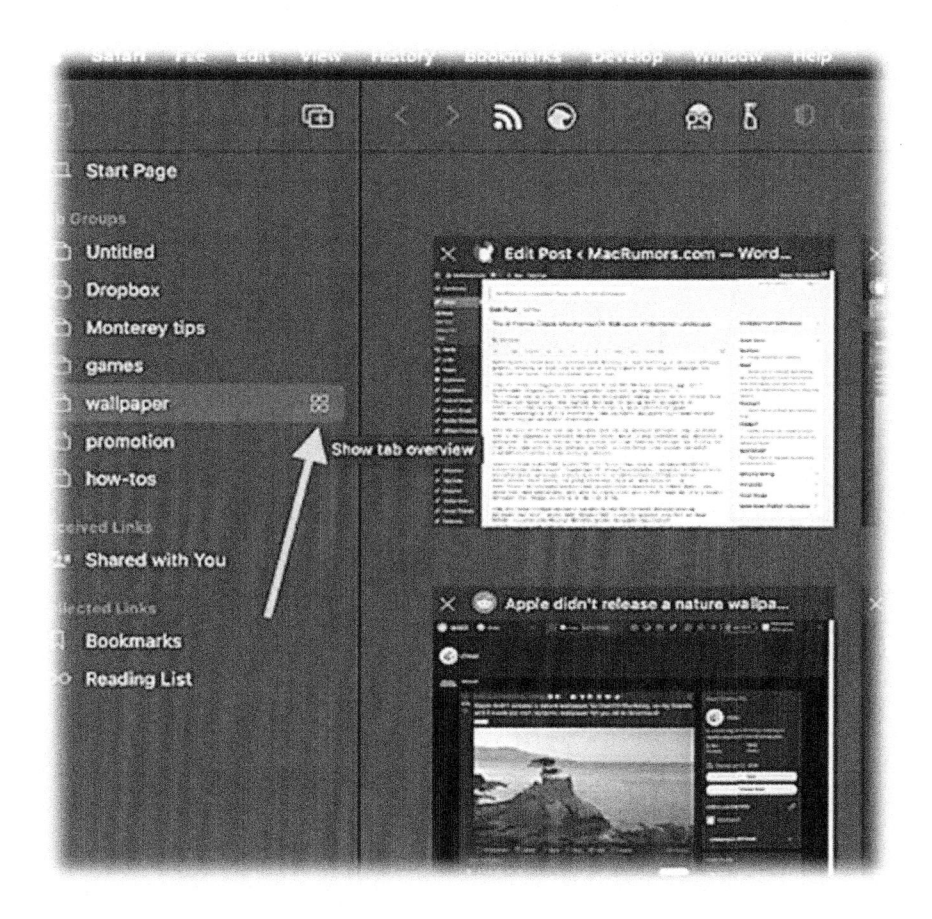

- To open the sidebar, choose the button like a pair of traffic lights and typing "Show Sidebar."
- Choose a Tab Group, and then click the 4 square icon.

You can also obtain an overview by right-clicking (Ctrl-clicking) the Tabs Group you're interested in and choosing Show Tab Overview.

Rearrange Tab Groups

- To open the sidebar, choose the button like a pair of traffic lights and typing "Show Sidebar."
- Simply click and press a Tab Group in the list, shift it to its new location, and remove hands from the mouse button.

Remove a Tabs Group

- Open the sidebar by choosing the Show Sidebar icon close to traffic lights and typing.
- Right-click (Control-click) Tabs Group and then click Delete.

Customize Safari toolbar

The Safari toolbar is where you should keep frequently used buttons. This includes everything from the Start menu to the Sidebar to the Tab View.

- First, you'll need to right-click the toolbar and choose "Customize Toolbar." After that, you can drop any item into the bar.

Drag your favourite items into the toolbar...

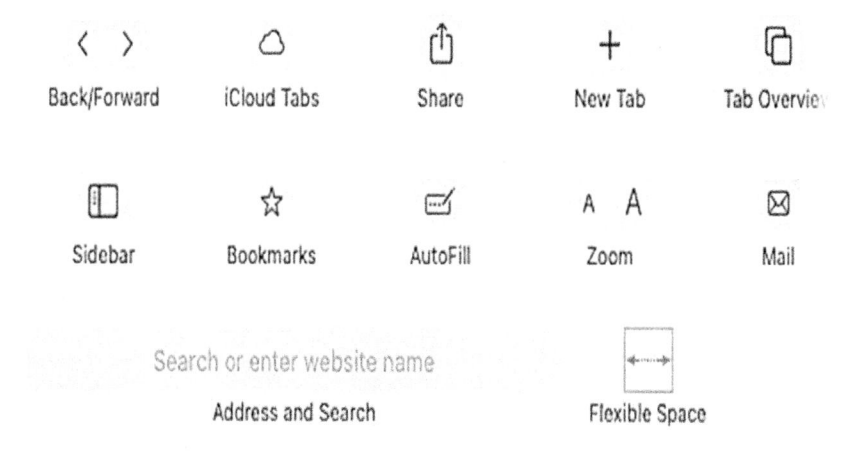

‹ ›	◯	⬆	+	⬚
Back/Forward	iCloud Tabs	Share	New Tab	Tab Overview
▢	☆	✎	A A	✉
Sidebar	Bookmarks	AutoFill	Zoom	Mail

Search or enter website name
Address and Search

⇿
Flexible Space

- Then, after you've got all the icons you need, drop them where you want them and hit "Done." Then, your modifications will be stored permanently.

Pick another search engine

- Select "Safari -> Preferences" to bring up the preferences menu in Safari.
- Select the "Search" tab.
- Third, a menu bar will appear, from which you can choose your preferred search engine (Google, Yahoo, Bing, Ecosia, or DuckDuckGo).

[Screenshot showing the Safari menu open with options: About Safari, Safari Extensions..., Preferences... (highlighted with an arrow), Privacy Report..., Settings for This Website..., Clear History..., Services, Hide Safari ⌘H, Hide Others ⌥⌘H, Show All, Quit Safari ⌘Q]

Newsletter subscription

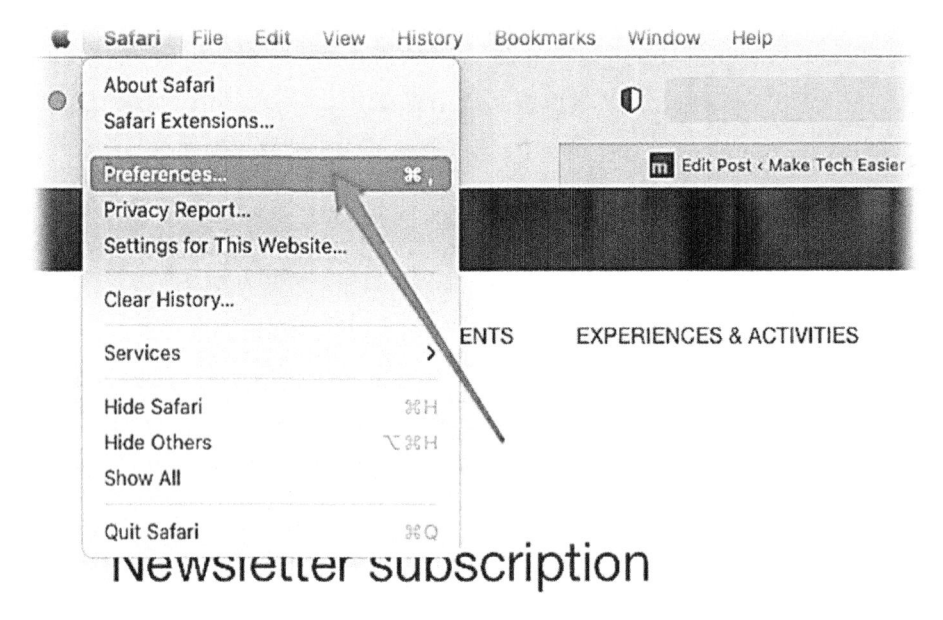

With the newsletter from Switzerland Tourism, you'll always be fully informed destination.

There is currently no option to integrate a custom search engine. For the time being, Safari will only support the most requested features.

Create PDF Web pages

Safari makes it easy to export web pages as PDF files. Follow these steps to export the current page as a PDF: go to the page you want to save; select File, then "Export as PDF."

- Select a location on your computer where you wish to store the page as the last action. You'll always have quick access to the PDF file inside Safari, Preview, or whatever PDF reader you want.

Safari Reading list

- The first option is to click the "+" symbol next to the URL of the site. You won't even have to take any action to add the item or website to your reading list.
- Alternatively, you can right-click the article and choose "Share," and then from the menu that appears, select "Add to Reading List." Choosing this option will add the selected item directly to your Reading List.

- To save articles for offline reading automatically, go to "Safari -> Preferences -> Advanced" before leaving for your flight.

Safari reader

- Click the four-line symbol to the left of the "+" icon in the URL bar to enable Reader.
- With a simple click, you can switch to Reader mode. If you click it again, you'll leave the reader mode.

Customize Safari's Icon

The Safari icon can be modified in a surprisingly simple manner.

- With the Ctrl key hold, click the Safari menu icon, and then choose "Options -> Show in Finder."

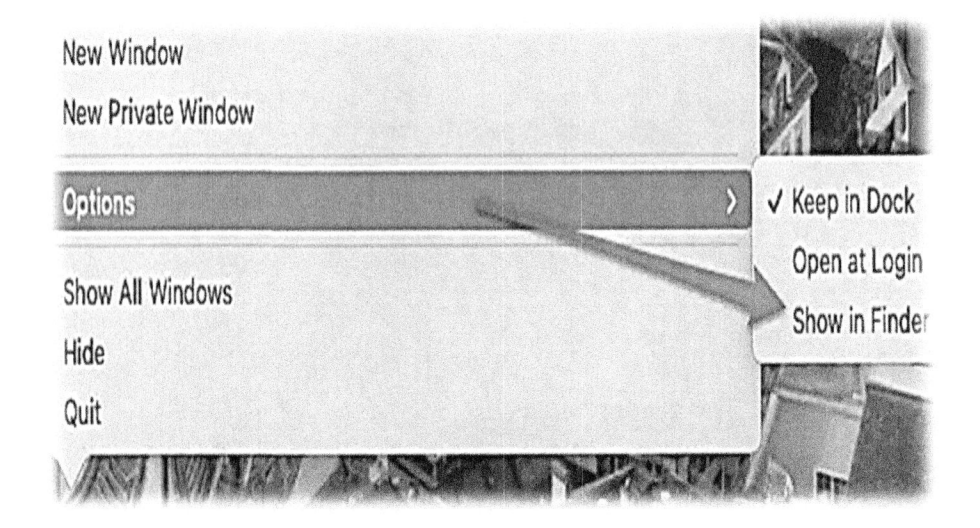

- Second, the Applications folder will be where you start when Finder launches. While holding Ctrl, click the Safari icon again, and this time choose "Get Info."
- A little Safari symbol adjacent to the "Safari app" can be seen in the upper left edge of the Get Info window.
- To change it, just click to select it and then drag your new icon picture into position.

Set Safari Background photo

Changing the Safari theme's homepage background picture is another option.

- To launch a new page with Safari, use the "+" button on the browser's upper right edge.
- In the lower right, click the symbol that looks like three stacked sliders.
- Click the "Background Image" checkbox to activate it. Select a personalized background picture from the gallery below.
- Safari allows you to use your own custom background pictures in addition to the pre-installed ones. Instead of selecting one of the other pictures, choose the "+" symbol.

- Select a picture to use as the background default in Safari.
- You should be able to view the results of your selection very instantly.

If you ever decide you need a fresh start, just right-click the desktop while holding down the Control key and choose "Clear Background."

Safari Homepage customization

- Hold down the Ctrl key and click on a page.
- Click "View as Icons."
- It's also possible to hide some of your most-used Favorites. Simply click on one of the "Frequently Visited" sites while holding down the Ctrl icon to convert them to icons. To implement your changes, choose "Delete" from the available options.

Safari Bookmarks Folders

- To begin, choose the icon in the upper left edge of the display, where the three colored circles are located.
- Second, while holding Ctrl, click anywhere on the bookmarks tab.
- Choose New Folder and name the folder.
- You can drag and drop pages into this folder.

Set up Safari Profiles

- Open Safari.
- Select System settings from Safari's menu.
- When the new window opens, choose Profiles from the top menu.
- Press the new profile on the information page that displays.

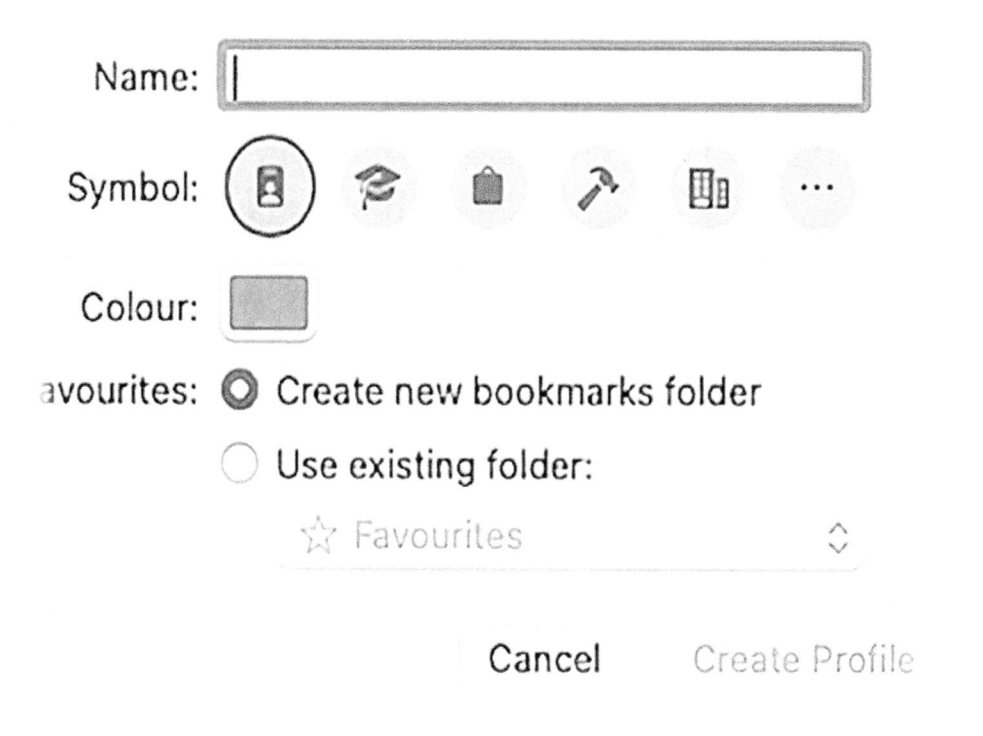

Set another Safari Profile

- Open Safari.
- Select System settings from Safari's menu.

- When the new window opens, choose Profiles from the top menu.
- On the left, you'll see your first newly added profile.
- To add a new profile, choose the + symbol in the lower left corner.
- Put in your details (username, preferred icon, etc.) on the same form.

Oddly, once you've made a Profile, you'll unlock two additional settings. If you choose its name, the old form with its name and icon appears again, but this time with tab and window management controls added.

- Like in the desktop version of Safari, you can set the Start Page as the default for new windows and tabs. However, this is also the profile where you can choose to manage Safari extensions.

How to use Safari Profiles

- In your dock, right-click the Safari icon.
- Select New Work Window or New Home Window.

Every action taken inside a Safari window within a Safari profile is saved only within that profile. This means that your bookmarks and addons can be kept private from other profiles. Here's where Tab Groups and Focus Modes in Chrome are like Safari Profiles. You may choose to enter a profile and hide all other content, much as in Focus Mode.

You can organize your work in distinct sections using Tab Groups. Already, Safari seems to just display the tabs you've designated as "Work" and nothing else while you're in a "Work" tab group.

Deleting Your Safari Profile

- Start up Safari on your Mac.
- Select System Preferences from Safari's menu.
- When the new window opens, choose Profiles from the top menu.
- On the left, you'll now see a list of all of your profiles.
- To choose one, just click.
- Go to the bottom left and hit the minus symbol.
- Verify by selecting the Delete Profile button.

Lock Safari Private tabs

- Start up Safari.
- Select Safari > Press Settings.
- Enter Privacy tab > Activate Touch ID required to view tabs.

Unlocking Safari private browsing

- "Private Browsing is Locked" will appear when you return to your previously opened Safari Private window on Mac. Then you can access the hidden tab with your Touch ID or password.

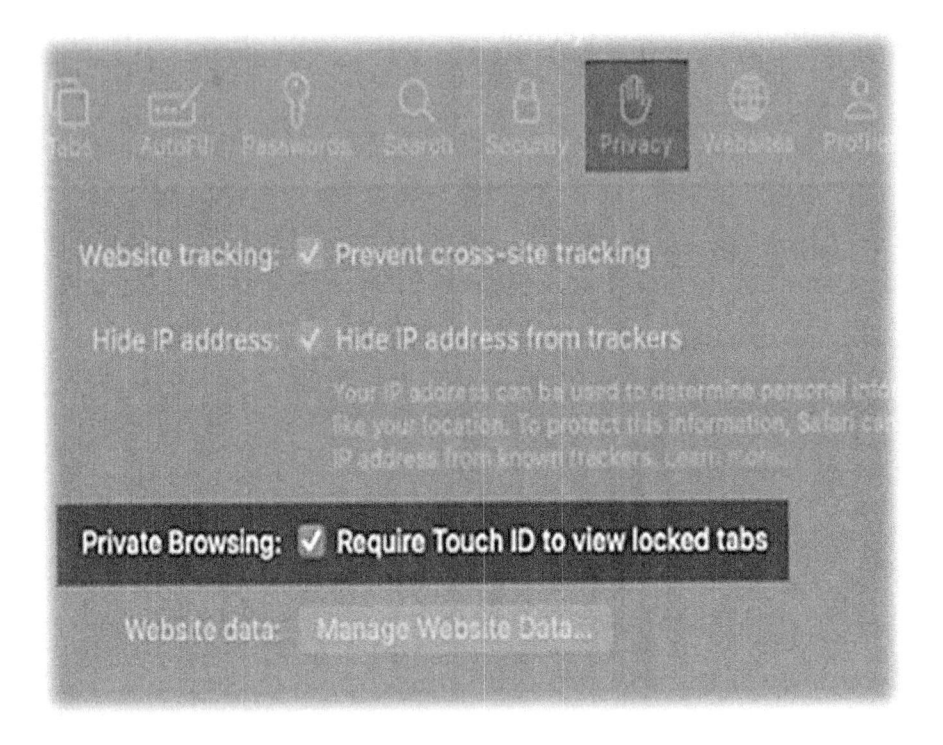

- After macOS has confirmed your identity using Touch ID or a password, you'll be able to resume using the Private browsing window.

- Find out who closed and opened the door.

Remove website tracking identifiers

- Launch Safari in the top left edge of your Mac, choose Preferences, then the Advanced tab.
- To enable this, click the box labeled Use Advanced Tracking and Fingerprinting Protection.

Then, choose all browsing from the drop-down menu.

CHAPTER 11

Create Template Reminders

- Launch the Reminders app and choose the list you want to work with.
- Pick File > Save as Template from the main menu.
- Renaming the template is optional.

Note that this is only the list's template's name, not your actual list.

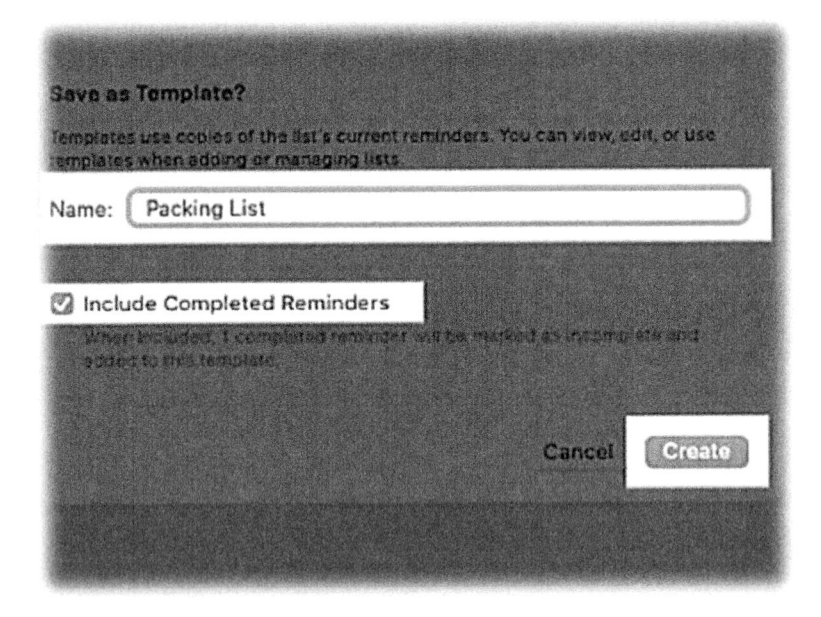

- If you wish to include reminders that have already been completed, use the box labeled Include Completed Reminders.
- To save a template, choose Create.

Use Reminders template

- Launch Reminders, then click Add List in the app's sidebar's footer.
- Enter the Templates tab.
- Make your template selection and then hit the Create List icon.

Share Reminders Template

- From the main menu, choose File > View Templates.
- Select Share Template by clicking the ellipses (...) next to the template.
- You will be notified to add Dates, tags, and places in the template.
- Select the items you prefer to include by checking the boxes close to them, then click the Continue icon.
- Follow the on-display directions after choosing a sharing method.

How to use Shopping reminders

- Launch the Mac's Reminders app.
- Choose the Add to List option.
- Label your grocery list.
- Select Shopping from the List Type menu.
- Choose an alternate list color and icon if desired.

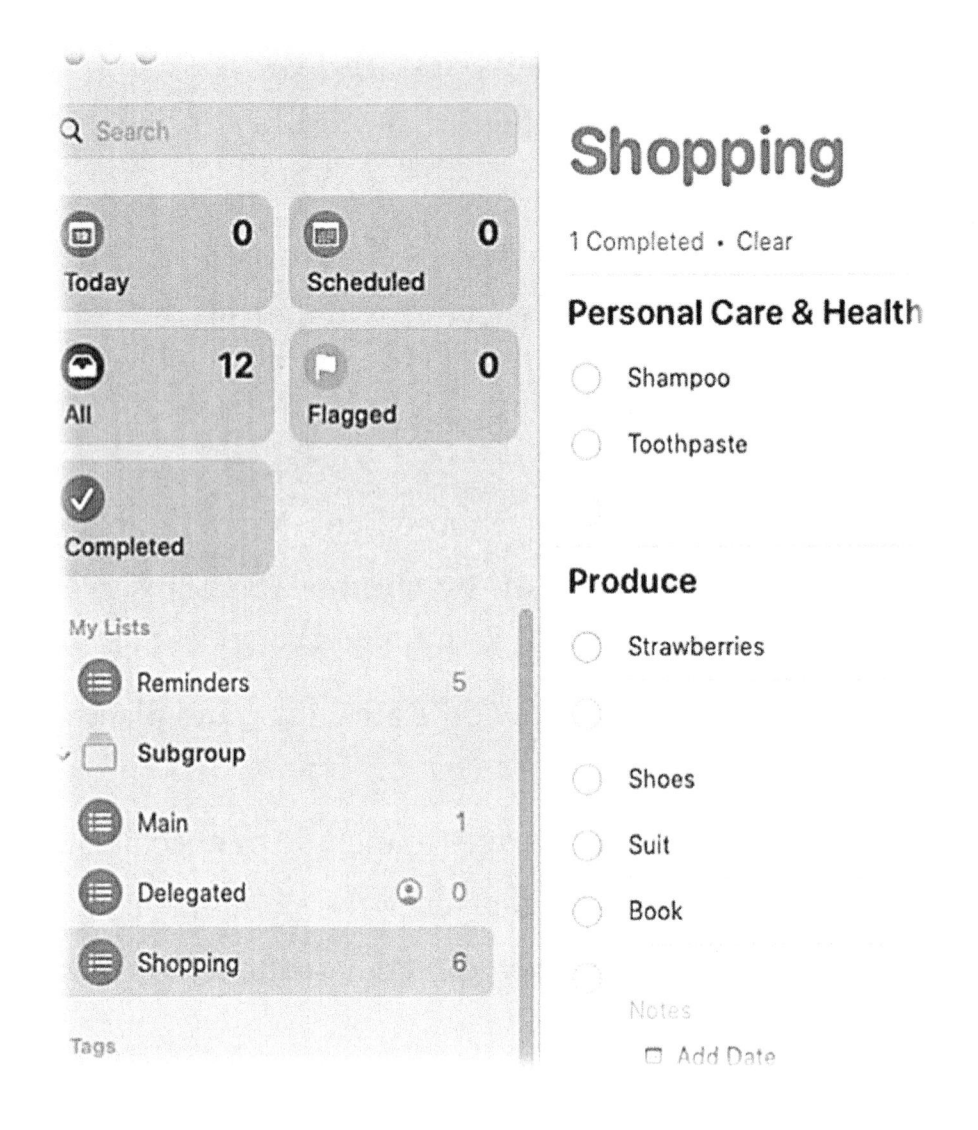

Well, I guess that's it then. There is no more configuration required; just begin entering your list of items to purchase.

Until a recognized item is entered, no subheadings will appear. It's a shocking development. Because it is not about a certain order, but rather about categories, the very first thing you include in the list is also sorted.

"Smart List Example" Info

Name: Smart List Example

Colour: ● ● ○ ● ● ◉   Icon: 😀 ☰
● ● ● ● ● ○

Include reminders matching [all ⇅] of the following filters:

Tags	⇅	All Selected	⇅
Date	⇅	Today	⇅
Time	⇅	Any	⇅
Priority	⇅	High	⇅
Flag	⇅	Flagged	⇅
Location	⇅	Specific	⇅	Greenhouse
Lists	⇅	Exclude Selected List	⇅	● Holiday

So if you press the plus symbol to create a new task and then input "Tomatoes," the instant you click Return, it gets filed under "Produce." Until you add data that fits a certain category, you won't see any of those categories or the associated tasks underneath them. If you search for "Perfume," for example, a new subcategory called "Personal Care & Health" will appear. Even if you don't initially classify "Toothpaste" as "Dental Care," it will be placed there the moment you save your list.

How to use Zoom Presenter Overlay

Using Presenter Overlay in macOS Sonoma, you can become a weather presenter during video chats or maintain eye contact with your audience while presenting slides. The procedure is as follows.

- Open Zoom
- Begin a call.
- Press the menu bar symbol and, if required, the video app name.
- Zoom's Share Screen option can be accessed from the main menu.
- Select "Advanced" from the Zoom pop-up.
- Slides as Virtual Background, and then double-click on it.
- Open your presentation in Keynote or PowerPoint.
- Press Share.

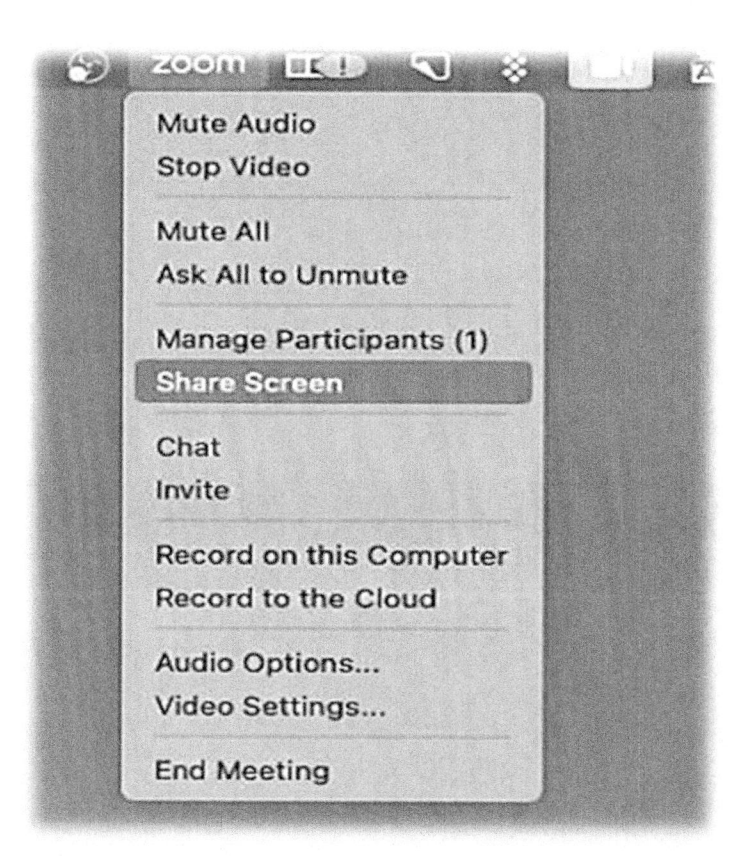

The display will then display your face and torso depending on where you are in the camera's field of view) but slides will appear in the backdrop.

Adjust the Presenter Overlay's size and position
- Select your face on the Zoom display.
- Simply drag to move around the frame.
- Or, to adjust the size, use the image's drag handles.

Then, choose Stop Sharing from the menu bar at the upper part of the display to exit Presenter Overlay. If you do that, the slides will disappear, and you'll once again see yourself in your natural environment.

Keynote Slide Transitions

The main advantages of using Keynote to create a presentation are the transitions and animations it provides.

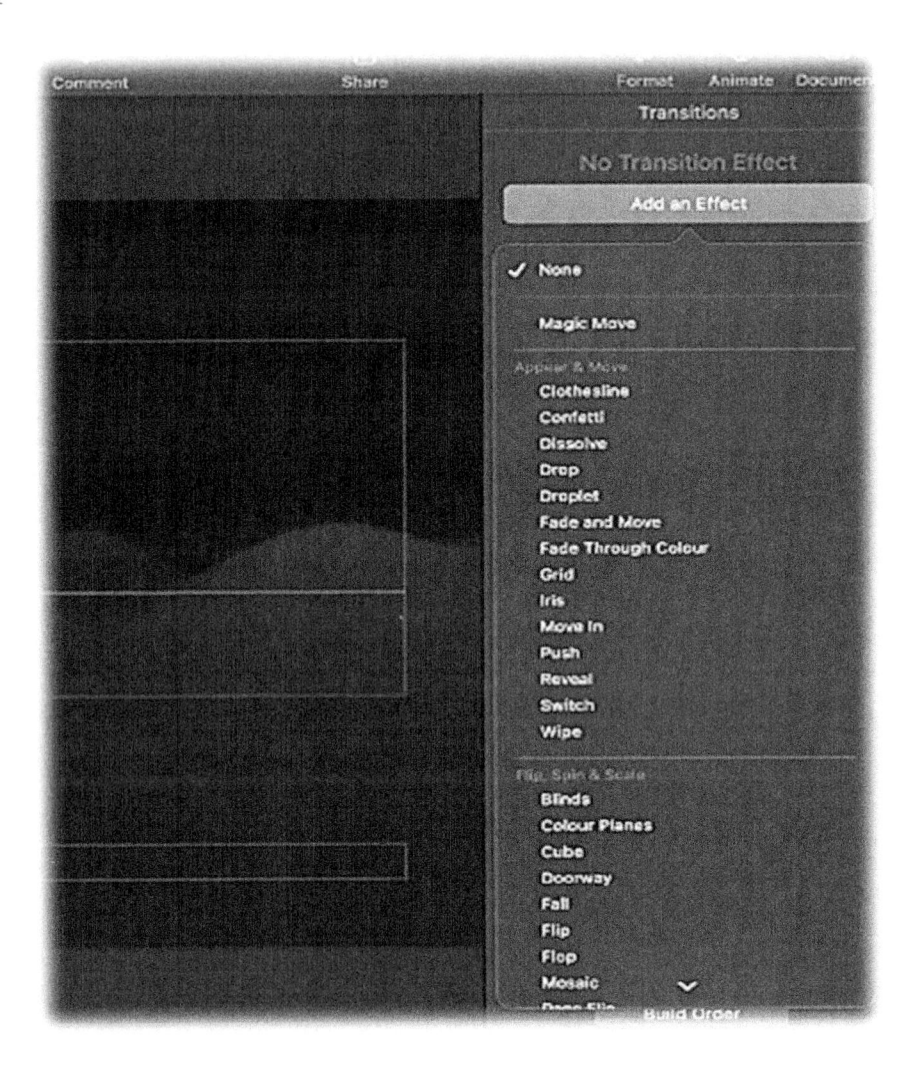

- Slides can be added to transition effects by selecting them from the left-hand slide navigator.
- Go to the upper right of the window to access the Animate tab.
- When you click on Action, a large blue Add an Effect icon will appear.
- There are more than a dozen options available when you click it. Here, we've implemented the Confetti effect.
- The timing, direction, and beginning point of a transition are all customizable once the transition has been chosen.

How to animate Keynote slides

You have complete command over when and where your items appear in Keynote.

- To add animation, click on Animate, then Build In, then Add an Effect.
- To see a preview, use the Preview icon. Select all of the items you wish to animate in sequence or simultaneously before specifying the Build In effect.

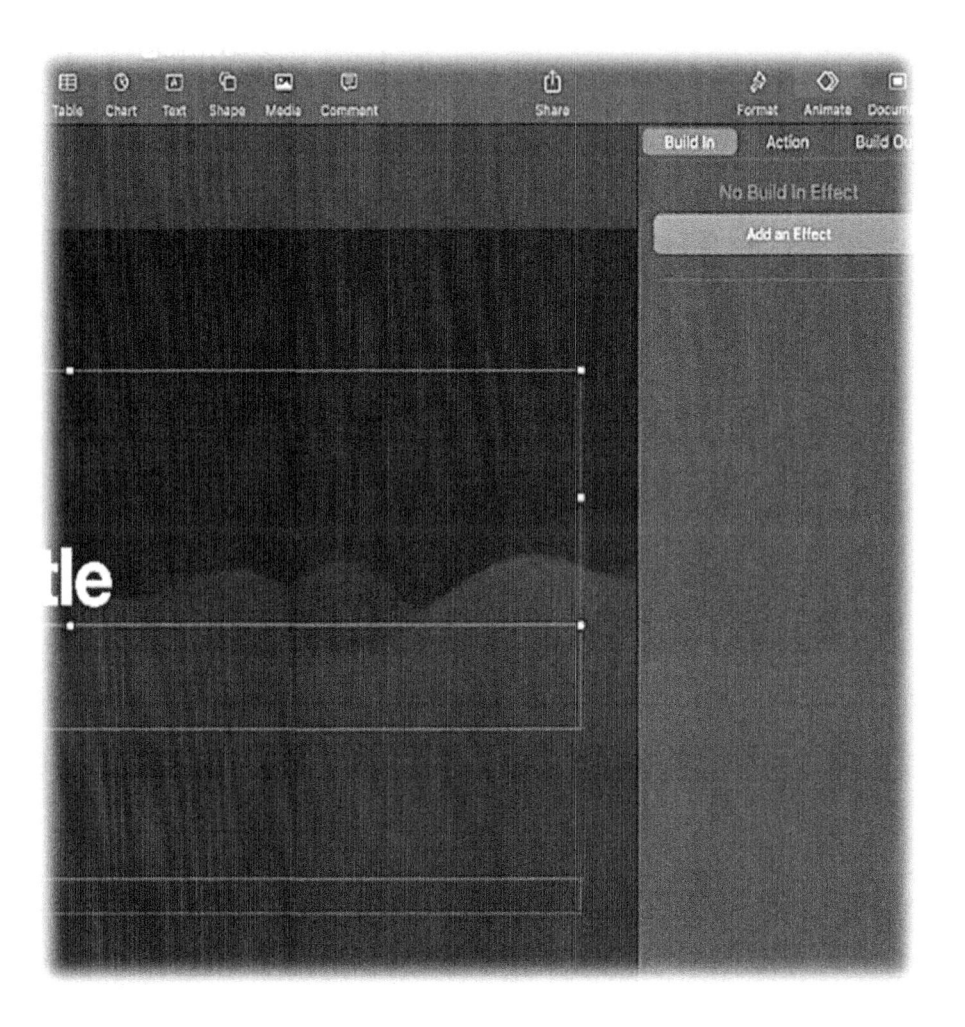

- When working with several items, choose the Build Order tab located at the sidebar's bottom. In this section, you can arrange how things show on the display.

Keynote Magic Move

With Magic Move, you can control the motion of a slide's item as you drag it from one to the next.

- Get the items where you wish to have them on the slides first. Press the Command + D keyboard shortcut to create a copy of the current slide in the Slide Navigator.
- Move the object around on both slides. Default settings for all items will be shown on the first slide. Arrange the components as you'd prefer them to be displayed on the 2nd slide.

- Choose just 1 of the 2 slides to animate and open the Animate panel in the sidebar.
- To apply the Magic Move effect, click the "Add an Effect" icon.

When you preview it, the transitions between slides are completely animated. The transition and animation are handled mechanically by Keynote. However, the time it takes to transition can be altered, and text can be used instead of physical objects if desired.

Edit Keynote Slide layouts

If you're putting up a major presentation, you should definitely use the same aesthetic throughout. This can be done by editing your slide layouts, a function that will help you specify the slide layouts and designs you use most often.

- It's easy to locate this function in Keynote. Keep the Control key on hold while using the trackpad to choose a slide on a Mac.
- Then, click the context menu item Edit Slide Layouts.
- Many aspects of your Keynote presentations can be modified by choosing Edit Slide Layouts. You can add a title, a picture, and a bunch of other stuff.

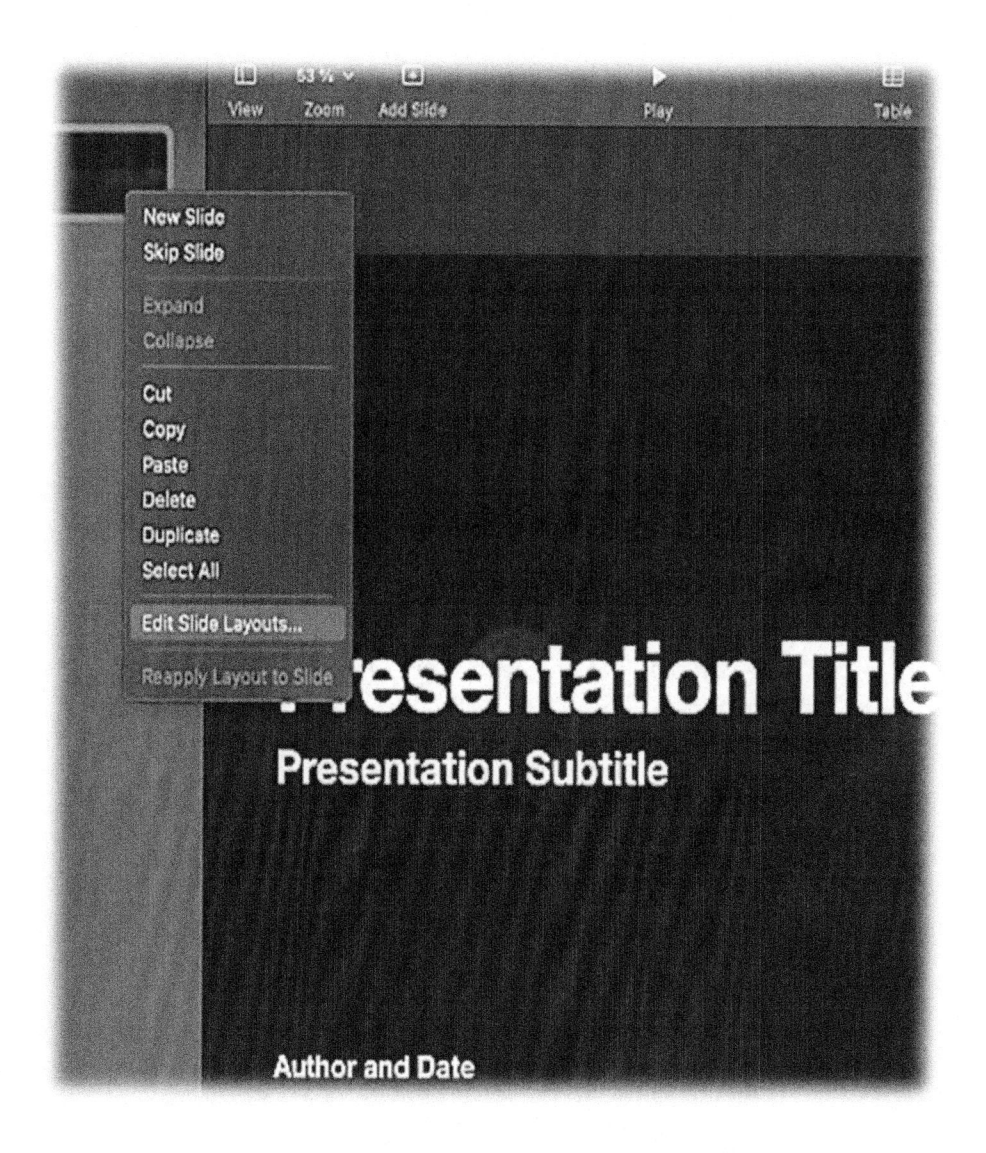

- When you're satisfied that it meets your requirements, click the blue Done icon at the bottom.

If you're not a fan of Keynote's presentation templates, you can always choose another option.

Customize keynote toolbar

Keynote makes it easy to personalize your toolbar.

- To change how the app's toolbar appears when you launch it from the macOS menu bar, choose View and then click Customize Toolbar.
- A new window will emerge, filled with a wide variety of movable icons and other components.

- Changing their positions is as simple as dragging and dropping your favorite functions, much as on an iOS device.

Select the Done icon in the lower right edge after you're through making changes to your toolbar.

CHAPTER 12

Safari Web apps

The ability to build web applications in Safari is all new in macOS Sonoma.

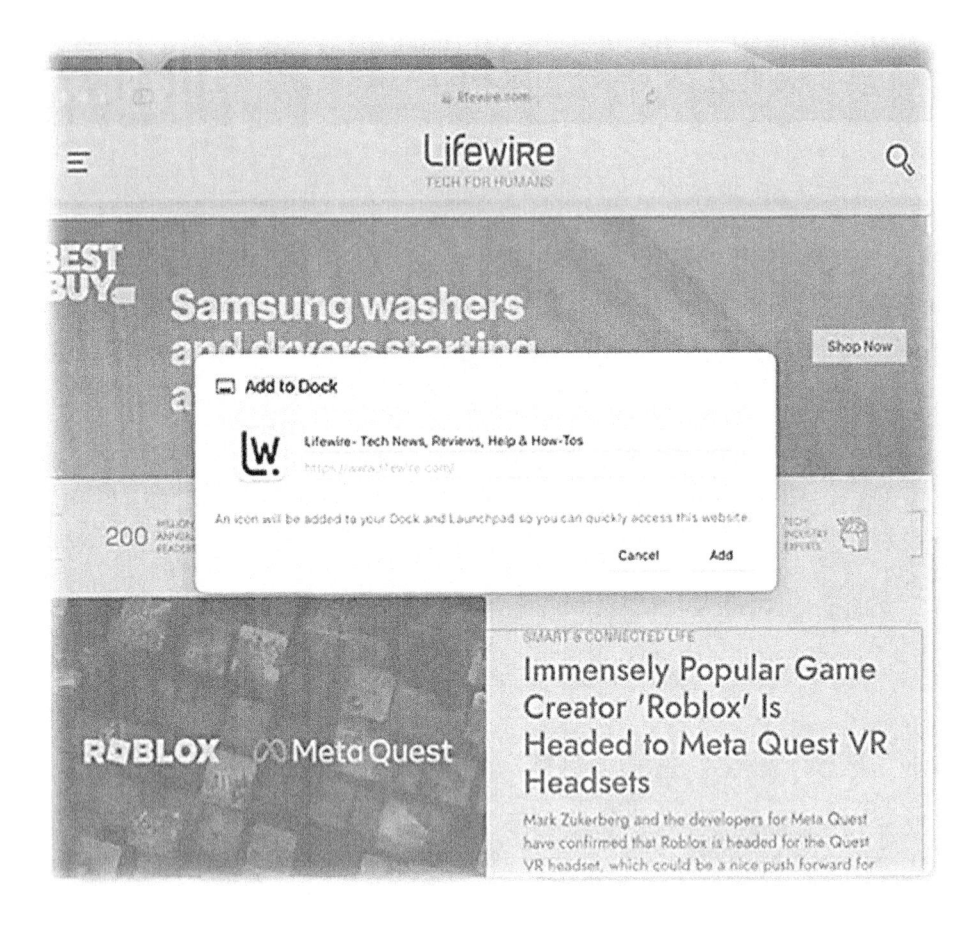

- When viewing a site, you plan to use often, select the sharing icon, then pick Add to Dock.
- This will be saved by Safari as a little app that will be placed in the dock. If you double-click the app's Dock

icon, you'll be sent directly to that page without any navigational tools or tabs.

- To access one of these online applications without having it appear in the dock, just drag its icon off of the dock. You can access them from your user folder by opening the Applications folder.
- You can save them to your computer's Desktop and then run them with a single click.

Both Spotlight and LaunchPad support launching them.

- Click the Safari menu item in the upper-right corner to open the page in Safari's main window.

Check Mac CPU Temperatures

- The Hot app is available for free on the iMazing website, approximately a third of the way down the page listing all available free apps.
- Go to the Applications folder by opening a Finder window. Then, transfer the Hot app by dragging it from the Dock's Downloads folder to the Applications folder. Either Launchpad or the Applications folder can be used to open the app.

- Locate the Hot app's flame-shaped icon on the screen's top menu bar. Right next to it will be the typical CPU temperature.

If you wish to change the Hot app's temperature display from Fahrenheit to Celsius, or access any other settings, use the menu.

Set up Hot Corners

- Open System settings.
- Select the Desktop & Dock menu item.

- To access the Hot Corners, scroll down and click it.
- The desired shortcut can then be assigned by using the drop-down choices in each of the four corners.

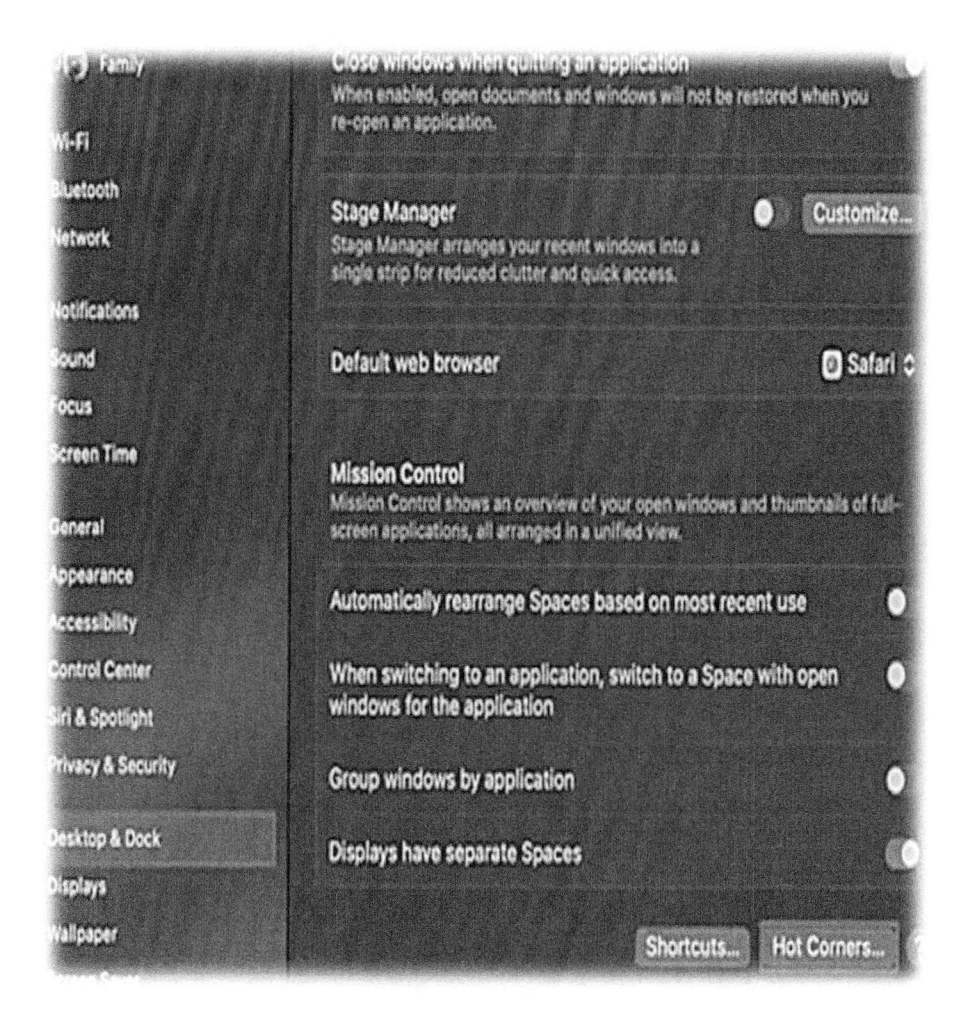

- When you're finished, click the Done icon.
- Simply moving the cursor to a Hot Corner will now cause macOS to act accordingly.

Those who depend largely on macOS for their jobs might benefit greatly from Hot Corners. This function can appear trivial to some people, but I use it often. I use one of the 4 corners to lock my Mac, another to access Launchpad, a third to check Notifications, and the fourth to see my desktop. My Mac no longer requires me to utilize the mouse or keyboard to do these tasks. Now you can access them with the click of a mouse.

Link AirPods to Mac

- While still encased, open your AirPods' lid.
- To activate the status light's white flash, press and hold either the setup button on the case's rear or the noise control button (on AirPods Max only).
- On your Mac, Select Apple menu > System Settings then press the Bluetooth in sidebar.
- Bluetooth headphones are superior to Apple's AirPods.
- Place the pointer over AirPods in the list of gadget on the right, and then hit the Connect icon.
- If your AirPods are compatible, you can activate Siri by saying "Hey Siri" and then clicking the Enable icon.

- When prompted to enhance Siri or Dictation, choose one of the following options:

Audio recording share: To give Apple permission to record your Siri and dictation sessions on this Mac, choose Share Audio Recordings.

Don't share audio: Press not now.

You can toggle the Improve Siri & Dictation option on and off in the Privacy & Security settings if you decide you want to start or stop sharing audio recordings.

Modify AirPods settings

- Go to the Settings Menu.
- In the left column, locate Input Device Settings and scroll down to it.
- If you've linked your AirPods with your Mac, they'll appear at the top of this area.

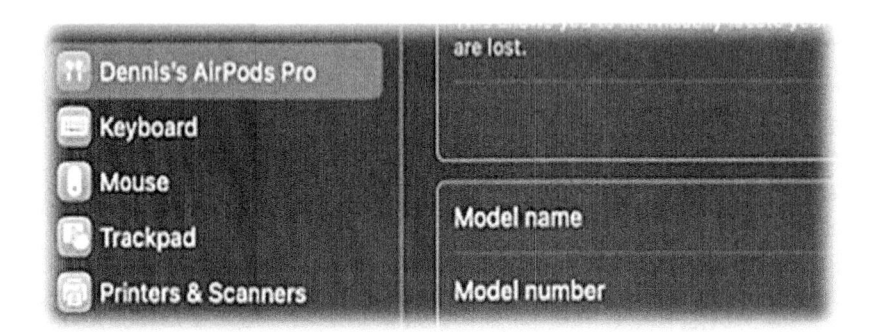

- You can now configure the AirPods' connection to your Mac when you double-tap Airpod, the Automatic Ear Detection, microphone settings, and more. If you're having trouble finding your AirPods, you can always use the Show in Find My option.

Connecting AirPods Pro (as seen) grants access to all the standard AirPods' options in addition to Noise Control and Spatial Audio adjustments.

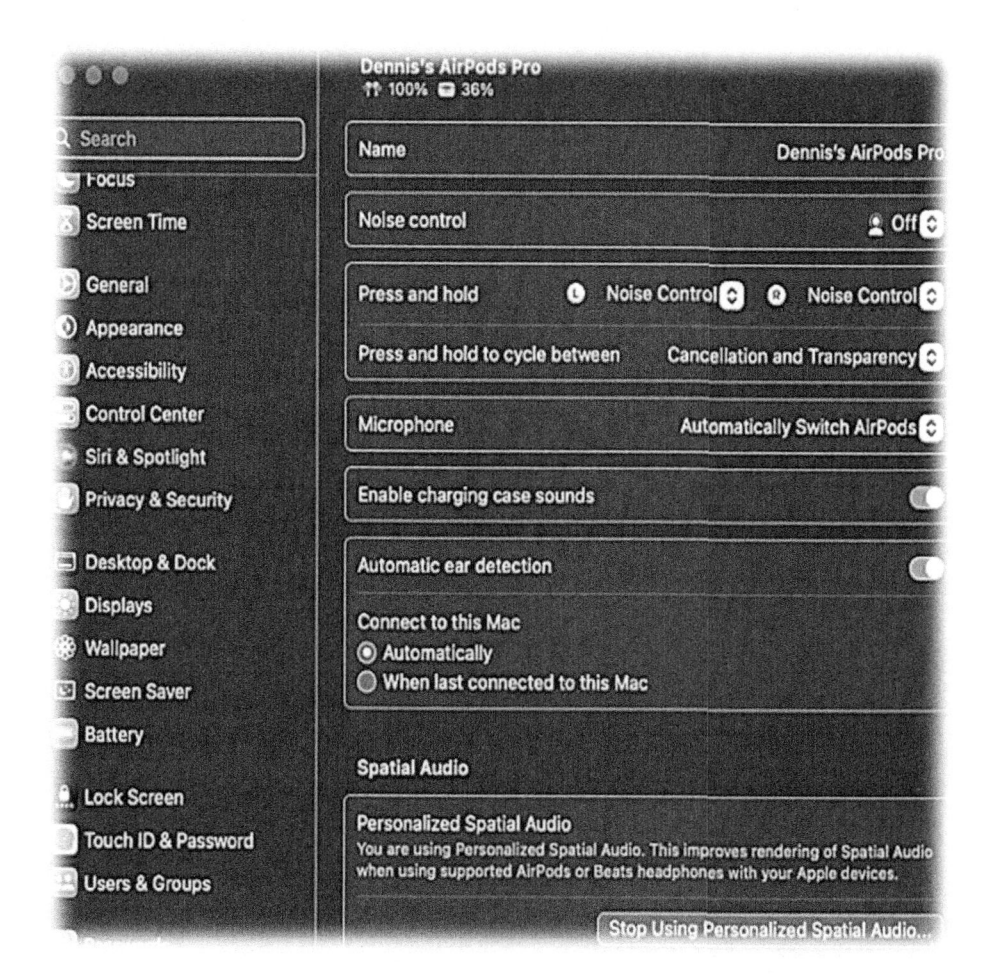

Activate Find My Location Services

- Enter System Preferences.
- Press on Privacy & Security.
- Unlock the configurations by clicking the padlock icon in the lower left. Type in your login information.
- Find Location Services on the left side of the Privacy menu.

- Enable location services by selecting the checkbox in the upper right edge.
- Select "Find My" from the right-hand list of applications.
- When you're done making changes, choose the Padlock icon.

To see all of the System Preferences settings, use the Show All button. This takes you back to the main menu where you can continue with the procedure.

Activate Find My

If you have already enabled Location Services or if you closed System Preferences, you will need to reopen them to activate Find My.

- Choose Apple ID.
- Choose iCloud from the menu on the left.
- Select "Find My" from the right-hand list of applications.
- If asked to give Find My Mac permission to access your location, choose Allow.

To enable Find My Mac and Find My Network, choose Options next to Find My on the right. To finish, choose the button.

- When done, close System Preferences.

Use Find My for friends and family

Find My allows you to track the whereabouts of people who have shared their location with you.

- Launch Find My.

- Go to the View > People menu item or the People tab at the top of the sidebar.
- Third, choose a contact from the list to view their pinpointed position on the map to the right.
- By clicking the Info icon next to their name on the map, you can find out their actual position with an address, obtain directions to their area, or add a notice.

Use Find My for gadgets

If you or a loved one loses an Apple device, the Find My app can help you locate it.

- Launch the Find My app.
- Go to the View > Devices menu option or click the Devices tab at the top of the sidebar.
- Choose an item from the list to see its position on the map to the right.
- On the map, click the info icon next to the device's name to get directions, play a sound, report it missing, or set up alerts for when you leave it somewhere.

Several shortcuts are available when you right-click a device in the list.

Search items with Find My

The Find My app also allows you to track the location of any AirTags or other things that are enabled for this purpose.

- Launch the Find My app.
- Go to View > Items or the Items link at the top of the sidebar.

- Identify its map location on the right by selecting the listed item.
- Tap the Info symbol close to the item's name on the map to view its precise position with an address, receive instructions to its place, enable alerts, or activate lost mode. What you can do with an item changes based on what it is.

Printed in Great Britain
by Amazon